The Rebuilding Workbook

Step-by-Step Guidance For
Healing When Your
Relationship Ends

Will Limón, MSW
With Nina Hart-Fisher

16pt

Copyright Page from the Original Book

Publisher's Note

This publication is designed to provide accurate and authoritative information in regard to the subject matter covered. It is sold with the understanding that the publisher is not engaged in rendering psychological, financial, legal, or other professional services. If expert assistance or counseling is needed, the services of a competent professional should be sought.

Distributed in Canada by Raincoast Books

Copyright © 2020 by Will Limón and Nina Hart-Fisher
Impact Publishers
An imprint of New Harbinger Publications, Inc.
5674 Shattuck Avenue
Oakland, CA 94609
www.newharbinger.com

Cover design by Amy Shoup

Acquired by Tesilya Hanauer

Edited by Gretel Hakanson

All Rights Reserved

Library of Congress Cataloging-in-Publication Data

Names: Limón, Will, author. | Hart, Nina, 1947- author.
Title: The rebuilding workbook : step-by-step guidance for healing when your relationship ends / by Will Limón, MSW ; with Nina Hart-Fisher.
Description: Oakland, CA : Impact Publishers, an imprint of New Harbinger Publications, Inc., 2020. | Includes bibliographical references.
Subjects: LCSH: Divorce--Psychological aspects. | Divorced people--Life skills guides. | Separation (Psychology) | Man-woman relationships.
Classification: LCC HQ814 .L72 2020 (print) | LCC HQ814 (ebook) | DDC 306.89--dc23
LC record available at https://lccn.loc.gov/2020019877
LC ebook record available at https://lccn.loc.gov/2020019878

Printed in the United States of America

22 21 20
10 9 8 7 6 5 4 3 2 1   First Printing

TABLE OF CONTENTS

Foreword — vii
Introduction: From Bitter Harvest to a Better Life — xii
    Chapter 1: Climbing the Rebuilding Blocks — 1

Part I: Surviving Abandonment — 18

    Chapter 2: Breaking Through Denial — 19
    Chapter 3: Conquering Fear — 38
    Chapter 4: Adaptation: Changing Relationship Patterns — 62
    Chapter 5: Overcoming Loneliness — 91

Part II: Healing Woundedness — 119

    Chapter 6: "Damage" Control: Unlovable, Guilt, and Rejection — 120
    Chapter 7: Cleansing Through Grief — 141
    Chapter 8: The Power of Anger, Part One: Releasing Anger About the Past — 170

Part III: Becoming Detached — 200

    Chapter 9: The Power of Anger, Part Two: Current Anger, Becoming Assertive — 201
    Chapter 10: Letting Go to Reach Forgiveness — 235

Part IV: Renewing Yourself — 268

    Chapter 11: Raising Self-Worth by Changing Self-Image — 270
    Chapter 12: Transition: Developing Identity — 301
    Chapter 13: Openness: Embracing Authenticity — 327
    Chapter 14: Uncovering Self-Love — 351

Part V: Reawakening to Life — 377

    Chapter 15: Building Friendships — 378
    Chapter 16: Exploring Sexuality and Trust — 408
    Chapter 17: Sharing Intimacy: Singleness, Relatedness, and Love — 433

Part VI: Reaching Wholeness — 463

    Chapter 18: Purpose: Accepting Abundance for the Journey Onward — 465

Chapter 19: Freedom, the View from the Mountaintop 483
Afterword 489
Acknowledgments 491
References 493
Back Cover Material 504

"Moving through divorce—and not getting stuck—requires conscious reflection and action. *The Rebuilding Workbook* provides seasoned guidance, laced with practical tools for self-reflection and next steps, as you do transformational work to gain new life and energy."

—**Sherod Miller, PhD,** codeveloper of Couple Communication

"As a child and family psychologist, I am pleased to endorse *The Rebuilding Workbook* by Will Limón and Nina Hart-Fisher as an invaluable tool for people that have experienced divorce. More than a simple fill-in-the-blank workbook, the author offers exercises, visualizations, and meditations to guide the reader on a path to healing. In addition, case vignettes and examples act as stimuli for thought and discussion. This workbook builds on Bruce Fisher's original book, and should be a required companion for any divorce adjustment seminar."

—**Daniel A. Doyle, EdD,** child and family psychologist

"*The Rebuilding Workbook* is an excellent resource for people who are suffering following a divorce or any other breakup. Through a series of thoughtfully constructed, compassionate, and engaging exercises, the authors provide expert guidance on how to manage painful feelings, and move toward a greater sense of hope and healing."

—**Mark S. Rye, PhD,** professor of psychology at Skidmore College, and coauthor of *The Divorce Recovery Workbook*

"I highly recommend *The Rebuilding Workbook*. Will Limón and Nina Hart-Fisher are introducing a new classic for anyone going through a breakup. 'Divorce alters your life,' and here is the path to guide your direction. An interactive learning style provides you with specific tools and exercises that can be used to address your past losses and future growth. It combines psychological insight with experiential learning, a practical approach that is deep and comprehensive. Indispensable for divorce recovery today."

—**Norm Gibson, LCSW,** former leader of Rebuilding Seminars in Boulder, CO, for more than twenty years; therapist with forty years' experience

"If you want to know *how* to accelerate your process of healing and moving forward after a relationship ends, this book is the definitive guide. Will and Nina combine clear explanations of the recovery process with meaningful action steps for moving onward. This book will help you navigate all aspects of the loss process, and lead you to new possibilities within the freedom to be yourself."

—**Bob Manthy, MA,** owner of Rebuilding Seminars in Boulder, CO

"Will Limón has a long career in helping individuals through one of life's most challenging times—a relationship ending. Will's insight as a therapist and facilitator of the Rebuilding process are reflected in his sensitive approach in the writing, as well as in framing questions and reflections. This book will help the reader progress even further in the process of disentanglement, healing, and transformation. This workbook will be a very helpful companion to *Rebuilding*, a book that has been the 'textbook' for the Rebuilding programs."

—**Nick Meima,** CEO of After Divorce Support, teacher of the Rebuilding program to hundreds of students worldwide, and pioneer of the online Rebuilding program

WILL—

To all the participants in my many Rebuilding Seminars. May these pages reflect your abundant courage, strength, and willingness to grow and share your humanity. I have learned so much from all of you.

To Dr. Bruce Fisher, my friend, who dreamed of making the world a better place and succeeded by helping so many people rebuild their lives, mine being one of them.

To my family, thank you so much for your loving support:

> My parents, Charles and Frances, passed on but never gone.
>
> My siblings, Charlene and John, companions in life.
>
> My son, Anthony, a bright light of enthusiasm and joy.

To my wife, Catherine, who continues to support my work, and shows me every day that the effort to have a truly loving relationship is the best work in the world.

NINA—

To my family. Your love, caring, and support continue to sustain me.

I'm forever grateful for those who have passed on:

My beloved husband, Dr. Bruce Fisher.

My remarkable parents, grandparents, and awesome brother, Dean.

My loving first-born daughter, Kelle.

My thanks for those with me now:

My dearest daughter, Kim, and her husband, Barry.

My cherished son, Dr. Robert Hart Fisher, and his wife, Katherine.

My precious grandchildren—Maddeson, Whitman, Keegan, Baden, Abby, and Deacon.

All of you remain in my heart.

Foreword

by Robert Alberti, PhD

How does he know exactly what I'm feeling?

In more than four decades as a psychologist, marriage and family therapist, author, and editor of popular and professional psychology books, I have known many, many therapists and authors who were influential and powerful in the lives of their clients and readers. None, however, were *more* influential, *more* powerful, or *more* downright practical than was Bruce Fisher.

And it was Bruce alone whose work brought readers to ask again and again, "How does he know exactly what I'm feeling?" Bruce knew because he'd been there. He listened. He paid attention. He studied the patterns that emerged from research with his *Fisher Divorce Adjustment Scale.* And he created a program—the program you'll discover in this workbook—based on what he learned.

This excellent update of Bruce's nineteen-step model for divorce recovery has been prepared by his two closest teammates. Will Limón was Bruce's first staff member in the Family Relations Learning Center, and taught the Fisher Divorce Seminar (now known as the Rebuilding Seminar) for over twenty years. Nina Hart-Fisher, Bruce's widow, co-led many of the divorce seminars Bruce gave internationally, and coauthored his *Loving Choices* book and workbook. There could have been no better choice of authors for this work. I'm delighted to offer this brief foreword as an invitation to you to read and benefit from it.

It was my privilege to have helped Bruce develop his lesson plan for a ten-week divorce workshop into the million-copy bestseller that is *Rebuilding: When Your Relationship Ends,* and to have played a part in keeping that book alive into its third and fourth editions. Perhaps you've read *Rebuilding,* or are reading it now alongside this workbook. Let me give you a bit of advice: Don't settle for just *reading* this material. *Use* the book and this workbook well. You'll take a few steps forward, then a step back. You'll progress better if you take part in the Fisher seminar. But whatever else you do, allow yourself the time it will require to work through the divorce process. Bruce's research showed that it can take two years or more.

Wait. What? *Two years?* I know that's not what you want to hear. But in the real world you won't go from married person to divorced person to fulfilled independent person in a few weeks, or even a few months. The good news is that you have in your hands a valuable tool—this workbook—that will help you through the process much faster.

One of the great things about a workbook is that it can be a sort of structured diary or journal—giving you space to keep track, forcing you to think about questions you might otherwise have avoided. Like a diary, nobody else sees it unless you want them to. You're completely free to record your answers and thoughts and fears and issues. Make it a powerful tool to motivate, structure, and record your journey and growth as you climb the divorce recovery mountain. Work through the exercises and action steps. Answer the questions. Fill in the blanks. Keep a *Journal to Freedom.* Write in the margins. Above all, be honest with yourself.

If you're using this workbook as you take part in a Rebuilding seminar, you'll find the class will set the schedule for you, and you'll be learning a great deal from discussions and sharing with others. If you're using the book on your own, you can set your own pace and tailor your focus to what's happening in your life at the moment. Either way, don't be surprised if you find yourself going back over material that is important to you as you make your way up the mountain.

This workbook starts out with an overview of the process, followed by support for the early going, when you'll likely confront bouts of depression, anger, and loneliness—the darkness before dawn. As you work your way through the book, you'll begin to let go of the baggage you've been carrying from the past, you'll start to recognize your own personal strengths and worth, and you'll once again risk trusting others and opening yourself to new relationships. If you keep climbing, you'll discover a life of purpose and freedom. The process probably won't be smooth, and your life may not follow the sequence of the chapters, but at each point along the way this understanding guide will be at hand when you need support.

Bruce Fisher loved the Rocky Mountains, and he took climbing as the inspiration for his rebuilding blocks. So prepare yourself for a journey. Pack up your energy, your optimism, and your hopes for the future. Put on a sturdy pair of shoes. The rebuilding mountain lies ahead for you. Get yourself ready for the climb.

—Robert E. Alberti, PhD, co-author of *Your Perfect Right*

Introduction

From Bitter Harvest to a Better Life

If you are reading this, chances are you or others you know are dealing with emotional trauma from divorce.[1] Few changes are as life-altering. With relationship loss, also lost are many hopes, dreams, and your perception of yourself in the world. You may be overwhelmed by emotions—grief, anger, guilt, rejection, and hopelessness. You may feel relieved that the relationship is over but confused as to why it ended or concerned that similar difficulties may happen again with someone else. Divorce can create stress-related physical illness, alcohol abuse, or drug abuse. Even functioning each day may prove difficult. Yet, if you choose to,

---

[1] "Divorce" represents all relationship separation or loss, married or unmarried, gay or straight, and much of this workbook applies to widowhood.

from this loss and *often because of it,* you can create a stronger, healthier self.

Know What You're Looking At

Divorce is an "acute situational crisis" bound up in the ending of a relationship between two love partners. While painful, recovery does not take forever. Research indicates a recovery time of two or more years (Fisher and Alberti 2016). It's different for each person. Two essential points to keep in mind:

1. The key to healing is working consciously on the recovery process.
2. The greater effort you make to recover, the more quickly your life will improve.

Without focused change, the passing of time tends to bury wounds rather than heal them. Inevitably, they'll resurface with another partner. That's why you need to work through the ending of this love relationship before beginning a new one.

Since life is a dance, it helps to know the steps. Divorce recovery is more than healing from pain. It's also a learning process for personal growth. For some, this crisis uncovers childhood and early adulthood problems at the core of all relationship difficulties. Recovery provides valuable opportunities to heal these. A number of people have said to me, "I wish I had learned all this ten years ago!" It's important to celebrate that you are learning it now. Perhaps you'll become like Joan, who said, "My divorce really hurt, but it's also the best thing that ever happened to me. I feel alive again. Part of me wants to send a thank-you card to my ex."

You may feel as if parts of you are dying. However, if you choose to climb the rebuilding blocks to recovery in this workbook, your pain will be more than the death of old ways. It'll also be the birthing pain of a new life where you'll learn to relate in healthier ways to others and to "God," or any other term you may use to mean the essential force of life. If you're not a spiritual person, perhaps you can trust the forty years of this program's results; put simply, it works.

A Few Words for Parents

There is great pain in watching your children or grandchildren go through divorce. I know. The best thing you can do for them is to heal yourself and share your healing journey in age-appropriate ways. I remember Abby, who told her kids, "I'm angry about what's happening, and I'm going to let it out!" Instead of blaming the children's father, she beat her pillow on the floor with loud grunts and groans. The children (there were five of them) pounded their pillows as well. After a while, a large pillow fight erupted. Later, giggling and exhausted, they all collapsed into a giant hug. What a great way to teach children that it's okay to be angry and how to let out the emotion safely. George hugged his two kids and cried as he told them about the divorce. They cried too. Later, he said he'd never felt closer to his children than at that time. It's normal to have grief and anger. Show your children how to deal appropriately with these feelings and all the other issues around divorce.

Children need a loving, stable parent who communicates clearly, is optimistic about life, and builds a routine they can rely on. During divorce, this is a tall order. But if you work through this workbook, seek support, and learn important tools, you can do it. However, don't get so caught up in your children's needs that you don't take care of yourself. We are instructed when flying to put on our oxygen mask first, then to put on our child's. In the same way, get the adult support and assistance you need to heal. This will put you in the best position to help your kids. Getting counseling for yourself and your children can also be an important step.

How to Use This Workbook

This workbook is multidimensional. It takes the concepts from *Rebuilding* by Bruce Fisher, EdD, and Robert Alberti, PhD, (2016) and provides a place for you to put them into action. Chapter 1 gives a brief overview of the rebuilding blocks to healing, the workbook's framework. Throughout, additional material will enhance your understanding of the loss process, promote emotional healing, and give specific action steps for improving your life.

In the remaining chapters, the text contains a discussion of a particular rebuilding block(s) with unique exercises and assessments to help you apply the concepts to your own experience and construct specific plans for your life beyond divorce. These exercises will help you navigate all aspects of the loss process. Do whichever ones that apply to you. Over time, try them all for maximum healing.

Visualizations and meditations are available as downloadable audio files, which you can find on the website for this book: http://www.newharbinger.com/45397. These will help you heal by accessing other areas of your brain. They provide insight, encouragement, and instant support when feeling fear, loneliness, grief, anger, or other intense emotions.

"Journaling to Freedom" are spaces to document your passage through this difficult time. This invaluable record of healing and growth can provide lifelong inspiration.

"Will's Take" sections include specific suggestions, insights, and personal examples that I offer within the discussion.

"Nina Remembers..." boxes are personal reflections from contributor Nina Hart-Fisher, Dr. Fisher's widow. Nina and Bruce presented many Rebuilding Seminars and trainings for facilitators worldwide.

"Action Steps for Moving Onward" summarizes the exercises in each chapter and gives additional guidelines on how to heal and grow.

Mindfulness and Visualizations

Mindfulness has been shown to reduce depression and assist in both relaxation and coping with problematic situations (McKay, Wood, and Brantley 2007). It has been defined as "the practice of observing your experience in a nonjudgmental, compassionate, and accepting manner" (McKay, Davis, and Fanning 2011, 115). Guided visualization is a powerful technique to mindfully observe yourself and focus your thoughts on what you want to happen as if it were already an established reality. This creates an amazing energy that draws you mentally, physically, and emotionally toward your desired future. Here, visualizations will help you move through fear, loneliness, grief, anger, and other emotions, and the difficulties of loss to attain the wholeness and happiness you seek.

When visualizing, find a quiet place away from distractions. Allow yourself to breathe deeply to relieve stress and to enter into a focused state. Use your imagination to involve yourself with the situation or object being described, whether that's through sight, sound, touch, taste, smell, or vibration. Try "seeing" what the visualization presents, like when you close your eyes and images linger in your vision. If this is difficult, pretend to sense what is described in the visualizations. Soon, you may find no difference between what you pretend and what you actually perceive.

About the Author and Contributor

Author Will Limón, MSW. I first met Dr. Bruce Fisher in June of 1977. A friend had encouraged me to attend his divorce adjustment class. It had been over a year since my divorce, and I knew I had unresolved issues. So, I dropped in on the next session and was captivated by Dr. Fisher's presentation. Drawn to this family of folks healing from the loss of their love relationships, I joined the group. My life hasn't been the same since.

Bruce became my teacher, my mentor, and my friend. After the course ended, I volunteered in several classes as a small-group leader and used his concepts to teach a short divorce-adjustment program as part of my university coursework on mental health. Bruce encouraged me to join him, and I became the original staff member of his Family Relations Learning Center in Boulder, Colorado. For over twenty years I taught his seminar to thousands of participants along the Colorado front range. The program is still being taught in Colorado, throughout the United States, and in many foreign countries, as well as online. It's known as the Rebuilding Seminar from the title of his best-selling book, *Rebuilding: When Your Relationship Ends,* which has sold over a million copies since 1981 and is in its fourth edition, coauthored by Robert Alberti, PhD.

I am honored to present this workbook, drawing on what I learned from Bruce and from my experiences teaching the course. The contributions of Nina Hart-Fisher, Bruce's widow, are especially insightful as she was a key collaborator with Dr. Fisher on the Rebuilding Seminars. It is our joint desire that this workbook be an invaluable resource to assist your healing from relationship loss.

Contributor Nina Hart-Fisher. Soon after my beloved husband, Dr. Bruce Fisher, and I completed the last version of the *Loving Choices* book and workbook, Bruce became ill. During his last precious months, we had many conversations about our work together, especially about the need to update some of his wise and profound works on loss. Now, twenty-two years since Bruce passed away, the update is happening. This newly revised *Rebuilding Workbook* is my gift and fulfilled promise for Bruce, for our son Dr. Robert William Hart Fisher, and for you.

I am often flooded with heartfelt remembrances of teaching the Rebuilding model with Bruce all around the world. In the "Nina Remembers..." sections, I share some of my favorite case stories. What I learned from our teaching is that the Rebuilding Program works when you work it, and you are worth it.

Contributing to this updated *Rebuilding Workbook* by Will Limón is a dream come true for me. Will is a longtime trusted colleague and friend, a respected and inspiring teacher, and an author. I am honored, excited, and privileged to be sharing in this much-needed workbook.

May this workbook guide you in recovery, healing, and growth. As you begin this journey, please take really good care and be kind to yourself.

Now, as you begin climbing the rebuilding blocks outlined in the next chapter, life may seem totally confusing, the answers to your questions hidden, the future frighteningly uncertain. Learn to live one day at a time. Keep in mind the words of the German poet Rainer Maria Rilke (1943):

> [H]ave patience with all unsolved problems in your heart and to try to love the questions themselves.... Do not search now for the answers, which cannot be given you, because you could not live them. That is the point, to live everything. Now you must live your problems. And perhaps gradually, without noticing it, you will live your way into the answer some distant day.

From *Letters to a Young Poet,* translated by K.W. Maurer

Will's Take *Though you have a difficult journey to make, I know you will do it. You have joined company with over one million readers who have* *climbed this rebuilding-block mountain. I have every confidence in you. I will be with you every step of the way. Together, let's make this a time of real growth.*

Chapter 1

Climbing the Rebuilding Blocks

*What lies before us and what lies behind us are small matters compared to what lies within us.
And when we bring what is within out into the world, miracles happen.*
—Author unknown

STEPS ALONG THE WAY

1. **A Brief Tour of the Rebuilding Blocks—The Pathway to Healing**
2. **Where Do You Start?**

Before your love relationship ended, perhaps your life was happy or at least comfortable, predictable. Now, everything has changed. You sit in an empty apartment or collapse on a chair in your house, a once-familiar surrounding that seems strange. You might feel relief that your relationship is over. Even so, you may be confused as to how this happened. More likely, you feel sad, or angry, or devastated. Perhaps your divorce occurred some time ago, yet anguish from its loss lingers in your life. It wasn't supposed to be this way. All you wanted was love, nurturing, and companionship. But that's not how it turned out. How do you deal with it?

I know how. I've been divorced. And, as a counselor and educator, I've spent over twenty years teaching Dr. Bruce Fisher's Rebuilding Seminar, helping thousands of individuals just like you move through their pain and begin a new life.

Since the end of a love relationship can be just as wounding to those who were never married as to those who were, "divorce" in this workbook represents all types of love relationship loss, including being widowed, the loss of LGBTQ partnerships, and those who want to work at ending an old relationship to build a new one with the same partner.

I've counseled those who were abandoned by a love partner and those who walked out. Most wondered why it happened. Many blamed their ex-partner and wished they had learned long ago how relationships worked and hadn't gotten involved with that person in the first place. All wanted to move beyond the loss of that love and replace pain with understanding, hope, and the joy of a brighter future. This is not an easy task. But there is a path. *Rebuilding: When Your Relationship Ends* by Bruce Fisher, EdD, and Robert Alberti, PhD, (2016) describes a series of "rebuilding blocks" for working through divorce, a most effective framework for recovery. This workbook discusses these rebuilding blocks, providing additional insights and practical exercises to help you heal from heartbreak.

Regardless of its cause, relationship loss upends our lives because it requires change. Whether from a current loss or a relationship that ended some time ago, when you are in pain, recovery is a here-and-now task. This workbook provides guidance for both.

A Brief Tour of the Rebuilding Blocks

Your relationship loss is a watershed experience that will transform you. While the events of divorce will end, its lasting effects depend on the choices you make. You can make the best choices when you understand the rebuilding blocks to healing as described in *Rebuilding* and complete the exercises in this workbook. Here are the original rebuilding blocks. Several have added descriptions, which correspond to this workbook's exploration of them as outlined in the following discussion.

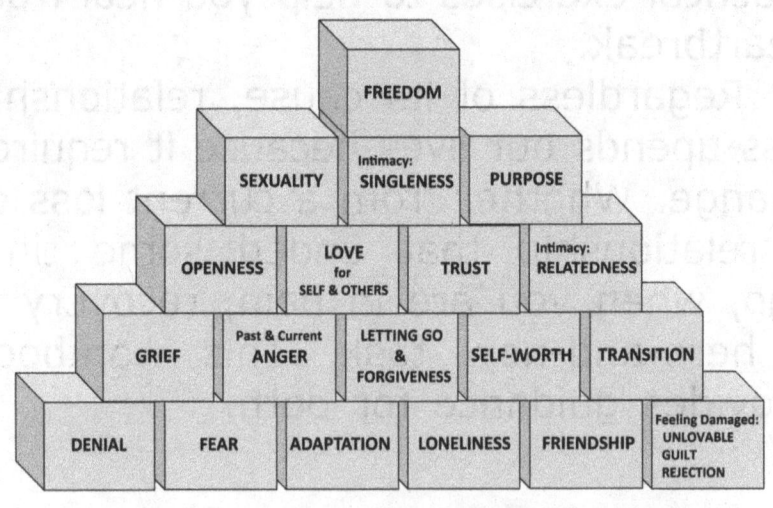

The Rebuilding Blocks to Healing

Drawing on my twenty years' experience teaching Rebuilding Seminars, I find it useful to organize the rebuilding blocks according to the following categories:
1. *Surviving abandonment:* denial, fear, adaptation, loneliness, friendship.
2. *Healing woundedness:* feeling "damaged" (unlovable, guilt, rejection), grief, anger (about the past).
3. *Becoming detached:* anger (about the present), letting go forgiveness.
4. *Renewing yourself:* self-worth, transition, openness, self-love.
5. *Reawakening to life:* love, trust, relatedness, friendships, sexuality, singleness.
6. *Reaching wholeness:* purpose, freedom.

You may note a few differences in this workbook from the original rebuilding blocks and their order in *Rebuilding*.
1. Friendship is discussed in two places, first with loneliness and then by itself. This is because

friendships reflect the relationship you have with yourself, which loneliness exposes, and the core of overcoming loneliness is building a good relationship with you. Friendship with others is discussed more extensively in a separate chapter.
2. Anger has two parts: first, how to deal with anger about the past, including the events that led to relationship loss; second, anger about present complications. The emotions are linked, but the strategies for dealing with them are different.
3. Forgiveness is presented along with letting go, for it's an essential process in your healing.
4. Love has two places: one for loving yourself, the other for building healthy love in intimacy with others. They, too, are connected as the love we give and accept is grounded in self-love. However, each deserves a separate discussion.
5. Two chapters in this workbook combine some of the rebuilding

blocks: sexuality with trust and singleness with relatedness and love (for others).

Here are the categories with a brief summary of their corresponding rebuilding blocks. Each chapter in the workbook will go into greater depth. While the rebuilding blocks are given in a particular sequence, know that they flow together. The earlier ones set the stage, and the later ones help you deal with any leftovers.

1. Surviving Abandonment

Denial. While denial is a natural defense against emotional overwhelm, you must open the door to the reality of loss and the feelings that come with it. This is essential to recover from divorce and to prepare for healthier relationships.

Fear. When you lack comfort in the present and lose hope for the future, feelings of fear arise. However, fear reveals what's most important, your attachment to life. The energy of fear also motivates you to change, not only to survive relationship loss but to thrive beyond it.

Adaptation. The reasons your relationship ended are often rooted in underlying childhood adaptation patterns. Changing unhealthy patterns will help you grow as an individual and as a love partner.

Loneliness and friendship. Loneliness can be devastating. Yet, it teaches important lessons about the most fundamental relationship: the one with yourself. Overcoming loneliness also helps you relate with others again and build strength for a new life.

2. Healing Woundedness

Feeling "Damaged" (Unlovable, Guilt, and Rejection). Though these feelings are real, you are greater than these emotions. They present tremendous opportunities for you to heal from relationship loss, uncover unhealthy relationship patterns, and overcome self-image issues.

Grief. If ignored, grief affects physical health and contributes to mental lapses or depression. When expressed, grief relieves stress and brings you closer to healing acceptance of your loss.

Anger (About the Past). As loss affects your life, anger can rise up suddenly or grow gradually. It often overlies grief, fear, frustration, and inadequacy. Used wisely, anger energy clarifies boundaries, builds courage, and helps protect you from other people and situations that provoke these underlying emotions. It also provides creative power to improve your life.

Will's Take No matter how deep your emotions, they are finite. When you experience them fully, their energy and your own drive for health will keep you going. If some resurface, you'll know how to deal with them. Most importantly, you'll know they won't last forever.

3. Becoming Detached

Anger (About the Present). Anger energy fosters assertive behavior where you stand up for yourself without infringing on others. This is important for divorce issues and in all areas of your life.

Letting Go and Forgiveness. Letting go allows you to leave the past and move on. Here, you remove leftover denial and release remaining grief and anger. Forgiveness doesn't mean that what happened is suddenly acceptable or forgotten. Rather, it's a gift you give yourself that frees you from the burden of loss.

4. Renewing Yourself

Self-Worth. Love relationships duplicate painful childhood interactions when negative self-images taught by parenting figures are reinforced by unhealthy love partners. When *you* define who you are, build self-worth, and reclaim life on your terms, you can overcome longstanding obstacles to joyful living.

Transition. With growing insight, you can transition from less-functional childhood messages by consciously developing your identity. With a deep sense of worth and personal acceptance, you'll be able to choose rewarding friendships and love relationships rather than replay old resentments, needs, and expectations.

Openness. Rather than feeling like a limited, unworthy soul, embrace your authentic self and find a wonderful, valuable, irreplaceable being of beauty inside you.

Self-Love. Uncover self-love by realizing the basic bond with yourself, the only relationship that's absolutely guaranteed. Promote that love through kindness and encouragement.

5. Reawakening to Life

Friendships. The natural extension of self-love is to establish healthy friendships, the best foundation for any relationship.

Sexuality and Trust. Beyond friendship, joining hands, possibly bodies, and maybe hearts can be frightening for many reasons: lack of experience, leftover divorce pain, fear of inadequacy, fear of disease, and fear of rejection are just a few. Build trust, first with yourself by being honest about thoughts and feelings and then by fulfilling commitments to yourself and others. Exploring sexuality, developing trust, and increasing your dating awareness can be very exciting and rewarding when you know how.

Singleness, Relatedness, and Love. Singleness is the celebration of your essence as a unique human being. Relatedness builds connections that help us thrive. Healthy love in any relationship—family, friend, committed partner—begins with healthy self-love that extends to love of another chosen in the context of connection and reciprocity. All of these aspects foster good parenting as well.

6. Reaching Wholeness

Purpose. Finding your purpose means opening up to what has always been an exquisitely bountiful life. You see how your growth would not have been possible without the motivation of relationship loss. Important questions challenge you to move in the healthiest directions.

Freedom. Realizing your strengths helps you define your freedom about what life will be.

Where Do You Start?

This overview should give you an idea where you are in the divorce-recovery process. Maybe you've already climbed some of the rebuilding blocks. If so, you may want to go directly to the rebuilding block that concerns you the most. However, be mindful of any emotions and issues you may have skipped. If you've not fully worked through them, they'll hamper your progress. Review the earlier chapters to be sure that you've learned what you need to know. If you're at the beginning of the process, each chapter will help you take the next step along the way.

At times you may need to return to a rebuilding block or emotion as new events bring up leftovers. If this happens, don't be discouraged. Conscious use of these healing techniques is very positive. And, while you may want to be healed right now (and who doesn't?), realize that it takes time. Purposeful steps will take you where you want to go.

As always, neither this nor any other book can replace the assistance of supportive family, friends, therapist, relationship coach, or divorce-recovery support group. Always get the human contact you need to help you through this time.

Journaling to Freedom

Write a "bon voyage" letter to yourself as you embark on your healing journey up the rebuilding block mountain. Share your hopes, dreams, fears, and anxieties. Proclaim your willingness and courage to do what it takes to succeed.

_____
_____
_____
_____
_____
_____

Taking the First Step. By getting an idea of where you are in the rebuilding blocks, you've already taken the first step. Let's continue. The chapters in Part I, "Surviving Abandonment," will help you by breaking through *denial,* conquering *fear,* understanding *adaptation* patterns, and overcoming *loneliness.* This will begin your healing in earnest.

Will's Take *I remember the vast emptiness I felt when my marriage ended. More than anything else, I got better because I stayed with my emotions rather than avoiding them. I found that I wasn't swallowed up by the feelings. Rather, when I expressed them appropriately, I learned a great deal about myself and became free to move on. Don't be discouraged by the pain you feel right now. Remember, I and thousands before you have made this journey. All of us cheer you on.*

Nina Remembers... *Virginia Satir, the mother of family therapy, wrote the foreword to Bruce's 1980 book, Rebuilding. After meeting her, she became a mentor for me. Here's one favorite Virginia quote: "Life is not what it's supposed to be. It's what it is. The way you cope with it is what makes the difference." This brilliant understanding has sustained me through years of ups and downs. Here's another favorite: "We need four hugs a day for survival. We need eight hugs a day for maintenance and twelve hugs a day for growth." May her wise words support and sustain you as well.*

Action Steps for Moving Onward

Start in the right direction by taking these steps.
1. Share the rebuilding blocks with a trusted friend and discuss:
    a. What you've gone through
    b. What you currently face
    c. What lies in the future
2. Write the letter to yourself about your healing journey up the rebuilding blocks and share with a trusted friend or family member.
3. Listen to the Living in the Journey of My Life meditation, available at http://www.newharbinger.com/45397.[2] Post the following message, from the end of the meditation, where you can see it every day: "Today, I experience my loss as a challenge to be met. I grow from my pain." If you write it

---

[2] All meditations are from Will Limón, Beyond the End of Love: Beginning Again After Relationship Loss (Seattle: Amazon Services, 2016). Used with permission.

down several times each day, you will boost your healing process. Do this with any of the meditation messages that speak to you.
4. Celebrate this work by reading an inspirational book or taking a walk in the country. Create healthy rituals that respect your courage to heal!

Part I

Surviving Abandonment

The next four chapters will help you begin your healing journey by revealing the limited scope of divorce, providing a process to face its reality, and aiming you toward important lessons for positive change. They will help you survive feeling abandoned and give you hope and the skills to begin rebuilding your life.

Chapter 2 will help you move beyond denial into a realistic understanding of relationship loss and how it fits in your life experience.

Chapter 3 will teach you a concrete skill to limit and overcome your fears.

Chapter 4 explores the patterns beneath all of your relationships, why relationships end, and how you can make healthier ones.

Chapter 2

Breaking Through Denial

None are so blind as those who will not see.
—Author unknown

STEPS ALONG THE WAY

1. **Uncovering Your Denial**
2. **Dissolving Denial**
3. **Understanding and Acceptance**

It's natural but not animal, vegetable, or mineral. It's odorless, colorless, invisible, and something we all have: denial. Denial is "the unconscious defense mechanism of denying the existence of painful facts" (Pam 2018), a normal psychological reaction to unwelcome change. Like the dam that holds back a reservoir and allows only a controlled stream to filter through, denial keeps you from being overwhelmed by your mental and emotional responses to traumatic events. This is useful, for a while.

The danger of denial is that you may cling to it in an attempt to avoid an unwanted reality. Those who try only experience greater anguish and confusion as events in the real world inevitably intrude. Just as numbness becomes a throbbing ache that exposes the extent of physical injury, so your emotional hurt reveals the depth of your love wound. You need to live within the truth even if it hurts. *Though it brings distress, breaking through denial is the only way you start to heal.* While working in this or any other chapter, if strong feelings, such as grief, anger, rejection, or unlovability arise, go to the portion of the book that addresses those emotions. Be sure to return to this discussion of denial to continue your recovery process. And, as always, get support from a therapist, helpful family, or friends.

Uncovering Your Denial

Denial is expressed in thoughts, feelings, and actions. Some examples:

1. **You Deny the Reality of Relationship Loss**

    Thoughts: *This isn't happening.*

    Feelings: Numbness.

    Actions: Get no emotional or legal support.

    Possible results: Blindsided by ex-partner's legal actions. Overwhelmed and confused by other realities: financial difficulties, children's problems, enforced housing change.

2. **You Deny Resistance to Relationship Loss**

    Thoughts: *It's okay that my marriage is ending. I'm happy for my ex-partner.*

    Feelings: Depression (from repressed anger), false joy.

    Actions: "Give away the store" in divorce settlement. Help out partner's new love.

    Possible results: Become a doormat for ex-partner by taking care of children on that person's weekend, for example. Suffer health problems from repressed emotions of grief and anger. Endure financial hardship from unfair property settlement.

3. **You Deny Both the Impact of Relationship Loss and the Need to Get Emotional Support**

    Thoughts: *This doesn't bother me. I don't need help.*

    Feelings: Repressed grief and anger result in depression or hopelessness, alienation, loneliness.

    Actions: Remain aloof, isolated from others.

    Possible results: Emotional or physical illness from repressed feelings. Needless loneliness brings despair. Anger at others results in further isolation.

4. **You Deny the Ability to Recover from Relationship Loss**

    Thoughts: *I won't make it through divorce.*

    Feelings: Panic, fear, anxiety, hopelessness, helplessness.

    Actions: Lean constantly on friends and family.

    Possible results: Loss of friends and family who get burned-out by demands for time and attention. Possible loss of job and children. Forecast future psychological and emotional difficulties.

5. **You Deny Partner's Role in Relationship Problems**

    Thoughts: *It's all my fault.*

    Feelings: Self-hatred, despair, anger, inconsolable grief.

    Actions: Hide at home, constantly cry. Possible suicide attempts.

    Possible results: Quality of life destroyed not by divorce but by being over-responsible for it. Loss of job, children, possibly of life. Don't uncover partner traits that contributed to relationship difficulties. Likely to choose a future partner with similar unhealthy qualities.

6. **You Deny Your Own Role in Relationship Problems**

    Thoughts: *It's all my ex-partner's fault.*

    Feelings: Anger, blame.

    Actions: Fight with or stalk ex-partner.

    Possible results: Go to jail for breaking restraining order. Lose contact with children. Suffer emotional and financial hardship. Don't uncover personal traits that contributed to relationship difficulties and are likely to cocreate similar relationships again and again.

These are only a few of the many ways individuals have sought to deny their relationship loss. Do you recognize any? If so, know that your realization shows you're moving out of denial and taking the first steps toward healing. Right now, jot down some of the thoughts, feelings, actions, and results that relate to any denial you've had about your relationship loss:

Thoughts: _____
_____
_____
_____
_____
_____
_____
_____

Feelings: _____

25

Actions: _____

Results: _____

_____
_____
_____
_____
_____
_____
_____
_____
_____

Your reaction: _____

Now, let's start removing leftover denial and explore what that reveals.

Dissolving Denial

Denial is dissolved through awareness of what you actually experienced in your ended relationship. This is challenging yet also enlightening. Here is a question to help you: Why are you getting a divorce? A difficult question that brings home the reality of your loss. If you can, describe in simple terms. If not, leave blank and return after further exploration.

_____
_____

More profound questions are: Why did you get into this love relationship in the first place? Did this relationship really fulfill your desires? The answers to these questions dissolve denial. They also give you an understanding of why your divorce happened, which helps you accept relationship loss and begin learning what you may need to change in yourself to avoid a similar situation.

Evaluate the following factors (Fisher and Alberti 2016) to see if any were involved in your decision to create a love relationship with your ex-partner (1 = low, 10 = high):

Reason	Rating: 1–10
Loneliness	
Escape unhappy parental home	
Solve career problems or for finding a role	
Expectation that everyone marries (or is in a relationship)	
Because only losers are single	
Need to "parent" someone or be "parented" by another	
Pregnant, or caused pregnancy	
"Falling in love"	

What are your top two? _____
Your reactions: _____

These reasons are generic. None of them focus on a commitment to an individual who has unique qualities and shortcomings. Since a satisfying love relationship comes from the realistic appraisal of self and partner, you need to uncover the specific reasons why you began your ended relationship. This is the first step in building the skills necessary to make healthier choices in the future.

Let's go deeper. What were specific reasons why you chose this particular partner? (Examples: This person appeared as ... a good provider, attractive and sexy, kind, caring, helpful for my career, a good parent.) Were they fulfilled? If so, was that desirable? These answers heighten awareness and further remove denial.

Reason	Rating: 1–10

Which of these do you miss? _____

Which of these were unfulfilled? _____

Your reactions: _____

Now, create an accurate picture of what occurred within your ended relationship. Compare what you desired in your love relationship with the actual intimacy you experienced. Also, rate the intimacy during the last few months leading to its end. Recognizing the differences between these helps dissolve denial. And, when you recall why your relationship began and compare your desires with reality, you can begin to understand why you're facing its end. The following categories of emotional bonding are based on McGill's (1986) *Report on Male Intimacy.*

Comparison: Desired vs. Actual Intimacy

Rate the following on a scale of I (low) to 10 (high) and note the difference in ratings between categories.

	Desired	Actual	End

1. Time together

My love partner and I built a history together by:

   a. Frequently spending time together

   b. The length of time we spent together

2. Shared experiences and life view

My love partner and I agreed on:

   a. Thoughts

   b. Feelings

   c. Wants and needs

   d. Outside experiences

My love-partner and I had compatible:

   a. Interests

   b. Goals

   c. Friends

	Desired	Actual	End
d. Financial attitudes	___	___	___
e. Housekeeping standards	___	___	___
f. Trust levels	___	___	___
g. Spiritual beliefs	___	___	___

3. *Depth and effectiveness of interpersonal communication*

My love partner and I communicated as deeply as possible:

	Desired	Actual	End
a. About our thoughts (values, fantasies)	___	___	___
b. About our emotions	___	___	___
c. About our wants and needs (desires)	___	___	___
d. Through physical affection	___	___	___
e. Through sexual expression	___	___	___

My love partner and I were able to:

	Desired	Actual	End
a. Resolve conflict	___	___	___
b. Make joint decisions	___	___	___

4. *Exclusivity*

My love partner and I shared more deeply with each other than with anyone else:

	Desired	Actual	End
a. Physically	___	___	___
b. Intellectually	___	___	___
c. Emotionally	___	___	___

5. *Collective concern*

My love partner and I respected:

	Desired	Actual	End
a. Time together	___	___	___
b. Time apart	___	___	___

Your reactions: _____

_____

_____

In all relationships, change occurs and challenges partners to adjust.

Without flexibility and understanding, even positive growth can bring about the end of a love relationship. Whether planned or unforeseen, change will stress a relationship and bring out hidden difficulties. Consider which of these may have contributed in your divorce situation (1 = unlikely to have contributed, 10 = extremely likely to have contributed).

Change	Rating: 1–10
Personal growth of one or both partners	
Education	
Religious experiences	
Attitude shifts	
Illness	
Anxiety	
Anger	
Relocation	
Stress or trauma	
Job change	
Having a child	
Illness of child	
Child leaving home	
Death of child	
Stepparenting issues	
Partner having affair	
You having an affair	
You leaving partner to end emotional ties with parents (which your relationship represented)	
Partner ending ties with parents by leaving you	
External project (building house, business, hobby)	
Financial issues	
Addiction	

Now, choose the three most significant changes and reflect on how they affected your relationship:

1. _____
_____
2. _____
_____
3. _____
_____

Understanding and Acceptance

If the reasons for staying with your ex-partner were not healthy or if changes made the relationship unworkable, realize that divorce may be one of the healthiest steps you've taken in a long time. For a love relationship to work, it takes two people who are willing and able to create and maintain it. If that willingness and ability is not there in both partners, and if there's no desire to learn, then divorce is not a failure but a positive action to move on with your life. Many people have a hard time accepting this. They think, *I made my vows and commitments, and I should keep them at whatever cost.* Yet, if that cost is the loss of your own personhood, if that cost is the loss of a healthy role model for your children as to what love and marriage can be, then the price is too high.

Acceptance of your divorce may still be cloaked in vestiges of denial. The following chapters will help you understand your ended relationship, move through the emotions of loss, and determine what you must change in yourself to create healthier relationships. Throughout your journey up the rebuilding blocks, you'll be guided to behaviors that keep you grounded in reality. In each area, you will be challenged to break through any remaining denial.

Will's Take *You cannot live without making mistakes, I know I can't. Each time I slip up, I renew my dedication to learn from them. My motto: "I know I'm going to make mistakes in my life. Let them be new ones!"*

Nina Remembers... *A Hawaiian man shared his denial. He hadn't accepted that his wife chose to leave even though she'd said she never loved or even liked him. Someone shared a quote from Voltaire: "Friendship is the marriage of the soul." These words helped him realize the truth. "We were* *not friends and never had been,"* he said. *"I learned profound lessons from this mistake now that I am no longer denying what really happened. The best part? My kids have an even better and wiser father."*

Action Steps for Moving Onward

1. Complete the assessments in this chapter and consider how the results help you accept the ending of your love relationship. Discuss these with a trusted friend or therapist.

    a. Describe your thoughts, feelings, and actions, and the results of denial.

    b. Answer, "Why are you getting a divorce?"

    c. Rate the factors why you entered into a love relationship.

    d. Examine the reasons you chose this particular partner.

    e. Do the Comparison vs. Actual Intimacy Assessment.

    f. Rate the changes that may have led to the ending of your relationship.

2. Listen to the I Have No Denial and the Dangers of Denial meditations.

Both can be downloaded from http://www.newharbinger.com/45397.

3. Listen to enjoyable music, take a walk, or do some other nourishing activity.

Chapter 3
Conquering Fear

Nothing in life is to be feared. It is only to be understood.
—Often attributed to Marie Curie

STEPS ALONG THE WAY

1. **Exploring Your Fears**
2. **Specific Steps to Conquer Fear**
3. **Finding Optimism for the Future**

Fear helps you distinguish what's real from what is not and protect yourself from possible harm. Facing fear is a key test in your climb up the rebuilding blocks, and here you are, nose to nose with it right away.

What's confusing and frightening about fear is that often you don't know what to do, whom to trust, how long this will last, and where you'll end up. You may be tempted to climb back down to denial. But there's only one way to go if you want to heal: into the emotions of loss. Understand your fear so that you can, as Shakespeare wrote, "take arms against a sea of troubles, and by opposing, end them." The problem many individuals experience is not fear but their ignorance about it.

FEAR, the Great Impostor

Healthy fear helps you limit your behavior so that you protect your physical, social, and emotional wellbeing. For example, your fear of another love relationship helps you avoid romantic involvement while you heal your love wound just as your fear of a tornado keeps you well clear of its devastating power.

Other fears may appear authentic but are really phantoms of the imagination. Tolly and Peggy Dylan Burkan (1983) defined this type of fear with the acronym *FEAR:* false evidence appearing real. The key word is "false." This kind of fear is an emotional response to predictions of the future. It may cripple you with misleading interpretations and foster undue anxiety or erroneous actions. Examples:

- Worrying about the effect of divorce on your kids may prompt fears they'll not succeed in school, yet no problems have arisen.
- A new dating partner says something that reminds you of your ex-spouse, and you get afraid this will become a similar relationship and leave.

Let's get grounded in reality and examine your fears. Then, we'll take specific steps to conquer them.

Exploring Your Fears

There's no doubt that relationship loss has many challenges, both real and imagined. Become aware of your fears to determine which are realistic and which are not. Then, it's easier to confront them.

Here are some typical fears people report during divorce. (This list represents fears you may be experiencing. It's *not* meant to be what you should fear, nor is it meant to create a fearful mentality.) If you find fears listed that don't fit you, it could mean you're limiting your fears already.

Rate how these may be present for you 1 (low) to 10 (high).

	Rating: 1–10
I'm unlovable. I'm no good.	
Divorce is all my fault.	
I will lose all my friends.	
My family will be unsupportive.	
I'm afraid of:	
Rejection	
Anger	
Illness	
Lawyers or court	
Custody or property issues	
Being a single parent	

	Rating: 1–10
I will always be depressed.	
I will keep crying.	
I will always feel numb.	
I will always be alone.	
I will go insane.	
My career is ruined.	
I will lose my job from hurting.	
I can't provide for my child(ren).	
I will have no money.	
I will never attain financial goals.	
My partner may return.	
My ex-partner will confront me.	
Dating will be awful.	
My next love relationship will end in divorce.	
I will never have another love relationship.	
I will never have the child(ren) or family life I desire.	
My children will be damaged.	
My child(ren) will grow up and abandon me.	
I will lose my child(ren).	
I will never be able to trust my judgment about others.	
I will never be happy again.	

What are the top three? _____

Your reaction: _____

Notice how "will," "never," and "always" keep cropping up. These are key indicators about the nature of your fears. "Will" in any statement indicates that the feared event has not happened and may never occur. Your fear comes from *projecting* what might happen. The words "never" and "always" lead to predicting disaster or dwelling on extreme outcomes. They're two examples of *catastrophizing* and *overgeneralization* that paint the bleakest picture from which you feel fear.

Recognize that your fears indicate what and whom you value in your life:
- Love for your children is shown by your fears about the impact of divorce on them.
- Your sense of responsibility is displayed in the fears you have concerning financial matters.
- Your self-love is evident in your fears that you may lose the support of family and friends.
- Finally, your fears about the future indicate a deep desire to create a happy, healthy life.

These are important and life-giving values. Allow yourself to understand and celebrate them even though you're afraid because you believe they're in jeopardy.

Let's go back to your top three fears. For each:
- Trace back to the flawed thoughts that sparked these false fears.
- Find the positive value under the fear.

For example:

Fear: My children will be damaged from divorce.
Flawed thought: *This hasn't happened.* (Projecting into future.)
Underlying value: Love for my children.

Fear: _____
Flawed thought: _____
Underlying value: _____
Fear: _____
Flawed thought: _____
Underlying value: _____
Fear: _____
Flawed thought: _____
Underlying value: _____
Your reaction: _____

Fear focuses your attention and motivates actions. Use the energy of fear to move beyond the emotion and resolve issues before serious problems arise.

Specific Steps to Conquer Fear

Like imagined ghosts that vanish in the morning light, fears flee when you understand them and take steps to remedy the situation. It takes courage, fortitude, and risks to dispel them, but life is full of risks whether you act or not. Your task is to make prudent risks on track with your recovery. The following framework will help you.

Recall the acronym *FEAR* (false evidence appearing real) by the Burkans. They outline an extremely useful four-step process to deal with fear. Let's explore each step, and then apply the steps to a typical fear during relationship loss.

1. Honestly Examine Your Present Condition

Honesty is the only path to healing and true success. First, determine what needs attention and what's more fantasy than fact. Do this by (1) stating what you fear may happen and (2) describing the current state of the situation.

For example:

Fear: I'll lose my job because I'm hurting so much from this divorce.

Current state: I cry at work. Others say they're concerned about me. I still have my job.

An honest appraisal of the current state helps you see your fear hasn't come true. From this, you realize that your fear is only one possible outcome, prompting you to take heart about the future and work to prevent problems.

Take the top three fears you listed before and compare each with current reality. Do more as you need to.

Fear: _____
Current state: _____

Fear: _____
Current state: _____

Fear: _____
Current state: _____

How did that feel? _____
Did you find that some of what you fear is not anywhere near happening? Which ones? _____
_____
_____

Do this to all your fears to get a reality check and help you focus on what really needs attention.

2. Visualize What You Want
Turn fears around by visualizing what you want to take place instead. The Burkans recommend two steps to do this.
1. *Visualize:* "What's the worst that can possibly happen?" As you see these disastrous images flashing in your mind ... see yourself *accepting* them. Experience *in your body* what the sensation would be like if you were able to emotionally accept the unacceptable.
2. *Expect the best.* Visualize that you have already achieved what you want. *Feel* the experience of "winning" in your body. Hold on to that ... as you ... follow your

plan of action. When you are emotionally prepared for the worst and yet ... expecting the best, your mind relaxes into a sense of having "all the bases covered." Maximum effectiveness always results from maintaining this attitude.

(Reprinted from *Guiding Yourself into a Spiritual Reality* by Tolly Burkan and Peggy Dylan Burkan, 1983, 90. [Emphasis original.])

3. Choose a Plan of Action

With knowledge from your visualization of success, create a plan to make that visualization a reality. The Burkans say to start with the endpoint and work backward to where you are now. See how these three steps work in the following example.

Conquering Your Fears: Barbara's Situation

1. *Honestly examine your present condition.*

Barbara's fear is: "I'll lose my job because I'm hurting so much from this divorce." The current state: "I cry at work. Others say they're concerned about me. I still have my job." Difficulties may arise that could jeopardize her job, but they have not done so yet.

2. *Visualize what you want.*

First, Barbara visualizes a worst-case scenario in which she's fired for crying, illness, and work inefficiency due to divorce turmoil. She also manages to imagine what it would be like to accept this. Next, Barbara visualizes a successful outcome where she manages emotions about divorce and copes well at work and elsewhere. She also visualizes the steps to achieving success: joining a ten-week program for growth and emotional support and obtaining a good lawyer. Both visualizations—the fear coming true and of her success in handling the situation—help Barbara discover how much she values her career.

3. *Choose a plan of action.*

Through visualizing, Barbara realizes the importance of support and knowledge to recover from divorce and the necessity of skilled legal counsel. She creates a plan to accomplish these, working backward from her desired outcomes:

Desired outcomes:	a. Manage divorce emotions.
	b. Complete legalities of divorce successfully.
	c. Maintain employment.
Before that. Step 5:	a. Complete divorce-recovery group and maintain support friendships.
	b. Meet legal deadlines.
Before that. Step 4:	a. Participate in divorce-recovery group.
	b. Discuss wants and needs with attorney.
	c. Communicate about divorce recovery with boss.
Before that. Step 3:	a. Begin divorce-recovery group.
	b. Hire divorce attorney.
Before that. Step 2:	a. Research counseling resources through work, on the internet (such as http://www.rebuilding.org), and from personal recommendations. Find a counselor or group for divorce recovery support.
	b. Talk to others, search the internet, interview attorneys.
Before that. Step 1:	a. Meet with boss to discuss personal challenges; commit to getting support, separating work and personal issues.

Now, we're ready for the fourth step in the Burkans' process:

4. Follow Your Plan of Action

Without action, nothing changes. Your fear is less likely to happen, and you'll spend less energy dreading the future when you act to meet your needs. Also, purposeful action often brings unexpected help. As W.H. Murray (1951) wrote:

> [When] one definitely commits then Providence moves too. All sorts of things occur to help one that would never otherwise have occurred ... raising in one's favor all manner of unforeseen incidents and meetings and material assistance...(6-7)

"Plan your work and work your plan" is a lot better than worrying. Sometimes, what's most difficult is beginning to act. After that, things begin to flow. How does Barbara approach this?

4. *Follow through on your plan of action.*

In sharing her needs and locating helpful resources, Barbara risks rejection. Yet, having these appropriate discussions (with a boss who cares, with group members who are trustworthy) are necessary for success. Without these actions, there's a greater likelihood that her emotions would emerge inappropriately and sabotage her employment.

Let's work on conquering one of your fears.

Practicing the Steps

First, explore a fear using the Fear Transformation visualization (available at http://www.newharbinger.com/45397). Imagine the worst outcome possible and your acceptance of it. Then, imagine the best outcome and let your visualization guide you on how to bring it about. Keep in mind that acceptance of a possible undesirable result does not mean that it's okay. It only means that you imagine living with it without fighting against its presence.

Will's Take *This framework will bring you a growing mastery over circumstances in your life. You are taking charge. And, realize that as you* *conquer any fear, your ability to conquer them all is strengthened.*

Now, do the four-step framework for the fears you visualized.

1. *Honestly examine your present position.*

Take the statements you have already made and expand on them. Dwell on the fact that what you fear is *not* part of present reality.

    Fear: _____
    Current state: _____

_____
_____
_____

2. *Visualize what you want.*

From the Fear Transformation visualization, describe the worst-case scenario and your visualization of success.

    a. Worst-case scenario: _____

_____
_____

    i. What were your thoughts? _____

_____

ii. What were your emotions? _____

iii. Though difficult, how might you accept this outcome? _____

b. Visualization of success: _____

i. What were your thoughts? _____

ii. What were your emotions? _____

iii. What lessons or strategies were revealed? _____

iv. What values are beneath your fear? _____

3. *Choose a plan of action.*

Map backward from the desired outcome and plot your plan of action using ingredients from your visualization of success. Break down any major steps into smaller ones as necessary.

Desired outcome: _____

Before that (step 5): _____

Before that (step 4): _____

Before that (step 3): _____

Before that (step 2): _____

Before that (step 1): _____

a. Who can help you? _____

b. What are needed resources? _____

c. How do you contact these people or resources? _____

For each step, describe what you'll do, with whom or what, and when. (For example: work on the property settlement with my lawyer at 10:00a.m. on Monday.)
Step 1. Do: _____
With whom: _____
When: _____
Step 2. Do: _____
With whom: _____
When: _____
Step 3. Do: _____
With whom: _____
When: _____
Step 4. Do: _____
With whom: _____
When: _____
Step 5. Do: _____
With whom: _____
When: _____

4. *Follow your plan of action.*

As you put your plan to work, evaluate any portion by asking yourself:
    a. Is this helping me to meet my desired result? _____
       i. If so, how? _____

ii. If not, what can I do differently? _____

A. Who can help me with this? _____

b. What can I learn from this to make my life better? _____

This work can bring you more optimism in your life.

Finding Optimism for the Future

When conquering fear and overcoming the pain and complications of loss, it helps to know that you are not alone. While others may not always support you as you would like, many find that an affirming connection to a loving Higher Power or Benevolent Creation is essential to help reach recovery. Allow yourself to experience this connection. And, as you conquer each fear and build a better life, have these successes reaffirm your belief in a loving universe.

Nina Remembers... *At a weekend workshop in Iowa, one woman shared that she had lost her husband to divorce because she'd misused substances to block out horrific memories of childhood abuse. Now, clean, sober, and grateful for her 12-step program, she said, "I'm blessed. I've learned that I don't need to numb myself in order to live. Though fear still shows up, I'm no longer afraid to be afraid. As the 12-step saying goes, 'Courage is fear that has said its prayers.' The miracle is that fear is becoming my teacher and my friend."*

Journaling to Freedom

Write a letter to your fears. State your willingness to listen and learn from them. Proclaim your courage to conquer them and your desire to find optimism as you recover.

Your climb through fear won't last forever. You may find yourself caught up in lifelong adaptation strategies or feel lost in loneliness, perhaps your greatest fear. However, these issues open up rich areas for growth, which we'll address in the next two chapters. For now, consider these words often attributed to William Arthur Ward, which are so necessary for us to truly live:

Risks

To laugh is to risk appearing the fool.

To weep is to risk appearing sentimental.

To reach out for another is to risk involvement.

To expose feelings is to risk exposing your true self.

To place your ideas, your dreams before a crowd is to risk their loss.

To love is to risk not being loved in return.

To live is to risk dying.

To hope is to risk despair.

To try is to risk failure.

But risks must be taken, because the greatest hazard in life is to risk nothing. Those who risk nothing, do nothing, have nothing and are nothing. They may avoid suffering and sorrow, but they cannot learn, feel, change, grow, love, live. Chained by their certitudes they are a slave, they have forfeited their freedom.

Only those who risk are free.

Action Steps for Moving Onward

Share your work with trusted friends or a group and get support.

1. Do the assessments and exercises in this chapter:

a. Rate the example fears. Find the flawed thought and underlying positive value for your three top fears.

b. Determine the current state of your three biggest fears.

c. Choose a fear, listen to the Fear Transformation visualization (downloadable audio), and work through the four steps to conquer your fear.

d. Write a letter to your fears.

2. As you follow through on your action plan, reevaluate, and alter it accordingly with your goal in mind.

3. Use the four-step system to conquer other fears. Try working on at least one different fear each week.

4. Listen to the I Am Afraid meditation (downloadable audio).

5. Celebrate your growing ability to learn from and conquer your fears by nurturing yourself.

Chapter 4

Adaptation: Changing Relationship Patterns

Those who cannot remember the past are condemned to repeat it.
—George Santayana

STEPS ALONG THE WAY

1. **Understanding Adapive Behaviors**
2. **Revealing Your Relationship Patterns**
3. **Balance Yourself to Create Healthier Relationships**

If you could go back ten years, what would you change? When you learn from your relationship history, you have that marvelous opportunity, not for the last ten years but in the next ten and beyond. As children, we learned to get along using adaptation behaviors. These may have served us at one time, but now they can create problems in all your relationships. Evaluating these behaviors will help you break through remaining denial, understand why you're getting a divorce, and prompt essential change so you can build better relationships.

Understanding Adaptive Behaviors

Transactional analysis (TA) developed by Eric Berne, MD, (2010; see also Harris 2012) is an excellent framework to give you an in-depth understanding of adaptive behaviors and what you can do differently. This is especially useful for uncovering over-responsible or under-responsible adaptation behaviors, which are at the core of unhealthy relationships.

TA defines personality components called the *child, parent,* and *adult ego states* that were learned in family, school, and social environments. Let's be clear: these labels (child, parent, adult) are not about chronological age. They describe distinct attitudes and behaviors that can be either appropriate or inappropriate depending on their use. Each "speak" in its own voice. Your life is a product of which ego-state voice(s) you have followed. If you want healthier relationships, it helps to understand the characteristics of these ego states and choose different voices to guide you. We'll explore each ego state, including the positive uses and how being stuck in a certain state or combination of states creates unhealthy relationships.

Then, you'll work through some exercises to help change your patterns. Throughout, the term "grown-up" is used to refer to a person eighteen years and older to avoid confusion with the adult ego state.

The Child Ego State

The child ego state is divided into the *natural child* and the *adaptive child*. Each contains separate voices that promote specific behaviors.

Natural-Child Voices: Spontaneous and Irresponsible

We're all born in the natural-child ego state with a spontaneous drive to explore. Fully half or more of what we learn as human beings occurs before age six. Emotions are rooted in the natural-child ego state as well.

Positive effects on grown-up self. A healthy person chooses this ego state when being appropriately childlike and carefree, for example cracking a joke or taking an unplanned walk. One isn't spontaneous all the time; there are healthy limits: "A time for work and a time for play."

Unhealthy effects on grown-up self. Those who relate mostly from this ego state act like overgrown children. They can be fun at times but are often unreliable when constant spontaneity becomes irresponsible. A relationship with someone like this is frustrating because your needs go unmet while this "child" flits about searching for fun.

Adaptive-Child Voices:
Creative-Persuasive and Manipulative

By the age of two, children begin to understand rules: Wash your hands. Say please and thank you. The adaptive-child ego state develops as the child learns to work around these rules. For example, the child is creative when being persuasive while pleading for dessert. These antics can also be quite manipulative when coupled with half-truths or outright lies.

Positive effects on grown-up self. Creativity helps in problem solving. As relationships exist through negotiation, persuasiveness is essential.

Unhealthy effects on grown-up self. When stuck in the adaptive child, individuals manipulate to get what they want. They often have an excuse, blame others, and don't take responsibility. A relationship with such a master manipulator is difficult, be it with parent, sibling, boss, or love partner.

Which child voices did you hear from the following (natural, adaptive, both)? Give examples.

Mother: _____
Father: _____
Ex-love-partner: _____
Yourself: _____

The Parent Ego State

The many rules we learned growing up form the core of the parent ego state, which is divided into two categories, the *critical parent* and the *nurturing parent*.

Critical-Parent Voices: Particular and Over-Responsible Perfectionist

By six years, much of one's personality has already been established from parental lessons or inferred from parental behavior. The critical-parent ego state creates rules from these and uses them to construct conscience. Directives using "should," "shouldn't," "supposed to," and so forth establish guidelines for acceptable behavior and instructions on how to accomplish tasks. This develops an inner critical-parent voice that promotes discipline, responsibility, and striving to do one's best. Let's use the word "particular" to represent these characteristics.

The child who is punished by an overly demanding caregiver can learn to be a perfectionist. Here, the critical-parent voice becomes the inner critic that demands perfection but never finds it.

Positive effects on grown-up self. When using the critical-parent voice appropriately, people are particular in specific situations, for example the research chemist who's careful about mixing compounds to avoid blowing up the lab. Being particular also maintains moral standards, for example a spouse may be physically attracted to a coworker yet doesn't act on it because commitment to fidelity is stronger than temptation. (A spontaneous natural child might act quite differently!)

Unhealthy effects on grown-up self. Problems occur when the critical-parent voice takes over completely. For example, the research chemist comes home and expects everyone to behave in the same exacting manner as he or she does at work. This perfectionist attitude creates misery through impossibly rigid demands. Perfectionists are over-responsible in a futile effort to make things be what they "should" be. Often, these folks are stuck in their heads, unaware of their emotions.

Nurturing-Parent Voices: Nurturing and Over-Responsible Scared Child

How a child is physically and psychologically nurtured has a tremendous effect on his or her health. Research in orphanages uncovered the failure to thrive syndrome where infants can literally waste away and die if not given psychological and emotional nurturing in addition to physical care (Perry and Szalavitz 2010). Beyond a physical reaction, the infant defines self by how its cared for, in other words, "I must be a good person because Mommy and Daddy play with me and feed me," or "There must be something wrong with me because Mommy and Daddy yell at me and don't feed or play with me." Fundamental decisions about self-image and hope are rooted in such experiences.

No one receives perfect attention. For some, parental role models provided sufficient nurturing to promote well-being, acceptance, and trust in self and the world. Others came from families where basic needs were incompletely met, and significant anger, shame, and criticism were present. These children often learned to meet others' needs as the only avenue to acceptance. They assumed the caretaker role, becoming over-responsible for siblings and parents. Over time, this over-responsibility covered up the pain of having one's own needs ignored.

Underneath are scared-child feelings: mistrust of self and others and a sense of being unacceptable, unloved, and unlovable.

Positive effects on grown-up self. These are expressed through appropriate nurturing that doesn't take away from another's growth or inappropriately limits one's self-care.

Unhealthy effects on grown-up self. These grown-ups have a hidden scared child. Insecure, they constantly give to others to ensure they won't be abandoned, yet they have difficulty accepting nurturance because deep down they don't believe they're worthy. For example (true story), a family of grown children had to force their mother to accept Christmas presents even as she bought lavish gifts for them. Later, she'd give her unopened gifts to others, including her children!

Caretakers and people-pleasers acting from their nurturing-parent ego state can be very controlling because they decide what gets given. Whether from neediness, a belief of "knowing better," or misguided intentions, the result is the same. This over-responsible behavior leads to unhealthy and unhappy relationships. Stereotypically, the nurturing-parent role is the woman's job: always take care of your children and husband. (The man's stereotype is the critical-parent perfectionist: supposed to know all the answers and fix everything perfectly.) Of course, both men and women can be stuck in either parent ego state.

Which child voices did you hear from the following (critical, nurturing, both)? Give examples.
Mother: _____
Father: _____
Ex-love-partner: _____
Yourself: _____

The Adult Ego State

The adult voice begins to develop at ten months when a child compares thoughts and feelings with the actual environment.

Adult Voice: Appropriate (Detached)

Ideally, the adult coordinates parent messages (what was taught) and child messages (desires and feelings) with adult knowledge (experience of how the world works). This helps determine what is appropriate. This process works only when the adult is connected to the other ego states. If detached from either the desires of the child or the guidelines of the parent, the adult does not have sufficient input to make healthy decisions.

Positive effects on grown-up self. The adult ego state mediates the other internal voices to help make appropriate decisions. For example, consider the avid golfer on a beautiful Monday morning. The natural child wants to skip work and golf. The adaptive child wants to call in sick. The critical parent believes working overtime will lessen temptation. The nurturing parent wants to get a tee time for a friend. Since this person is independent at work, the adult decides: "I'll work through lunch. If I get enough done, I'll play a round of golf. If not, I'll wait until another day."

Unhealthy effects on grown-up self. If your adult is connected to your parent but detached from your child, specific tasks and nurturing of others may be done appropriately, but one's own needs for nurturing and fun may go unsatisfied. If your adult is in touch with the child but detached from the parent, then your emotional, recreational, and creative needs may get met, but proper completion of tasks and healthy nurturing of others may be overlooked. You can only make healthy decisions about what's appropriate when you listen to all your inner voices. If you're not sure, ask for help. That's how we learn.

Which adult voice(s) did you hear from the following (appropriate, detached, both)? Give examples.

Mother: _____
Father: _____
Ex-love-partner: _____
Yourself: _____

The image on the next page shows a summary of all three ego states and their voice parts.

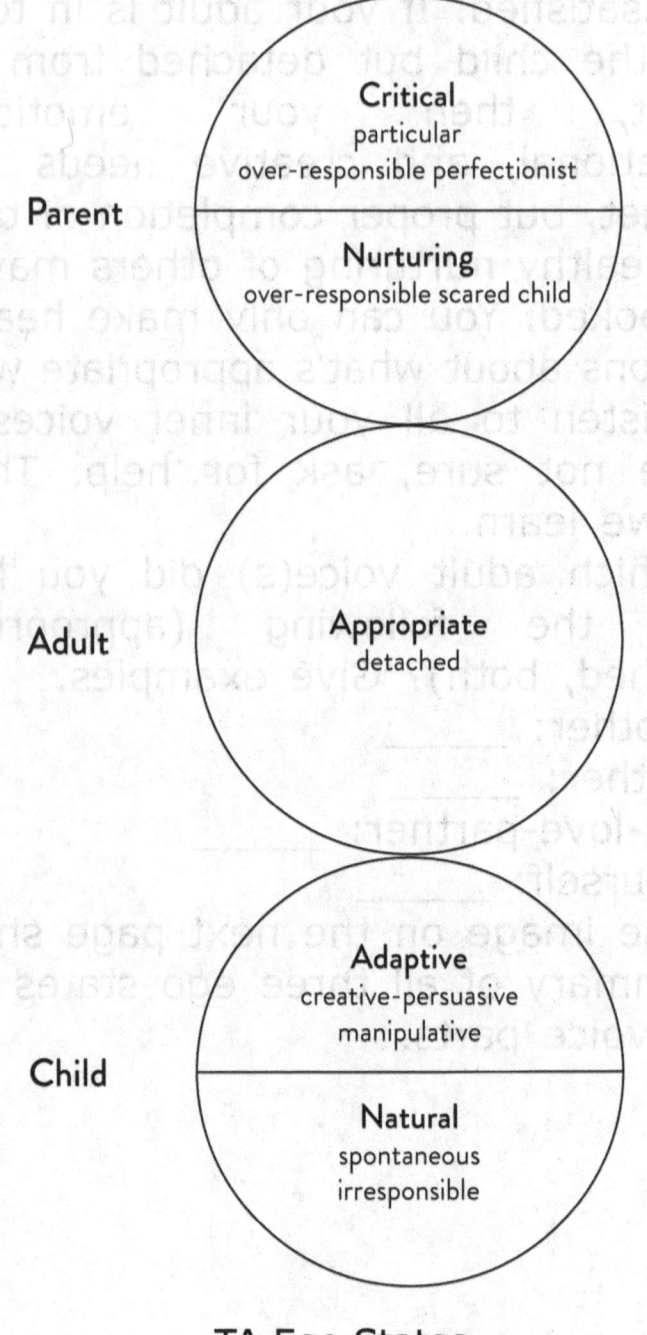

TA Ego States

How well you can identify the different ego states? Decide where each voice comes from: NC (natural child), AC (adaptive child), CP (critical parent), NP (nurturing parent), or A (adult).

1. "Do it again, correctly!"
2. "I never do this as well as you. Show me again."
3. "I'll help you at 2:00 p.m."
4. "I'm catching a movie. Join me?"
5. "Let me fix this for you. My project can wait."
6. "Sorry I'm late. Somebody always takes up my time."
7. "That'll never work. You should read the manual."
8. "That looks difficult. Need some help?"
9. "To heck with it! I'll never try this again!"
10. "I bought some perfect outfits for you on my shopping trip!"

(Answers: 1. = CP, 2. = AC, 3. = A, 4. = NC, 5. = NP, 6. = AC, 7. = CP, 8. = A, 9. = NC, 10. = NP)

Ego-State Combinations

Ego-state combinations are closer to real life. They can help you recognize individual personalities and the relationships they create. These combinations also reveal unhealthy patterns that may have been part of your ended relationship. Hopefully, this awareness will encourage you to change your patterns to avoid similar problems.

Here are combinations with examples indicating ego-state parts.

Nurturing Parent/Critical Parent

"Let me fix this for you because you won't learn how!"

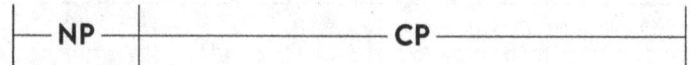

"I'll do this, but only once more, until you screw it up again."

Critical Parent/Adaptive Child

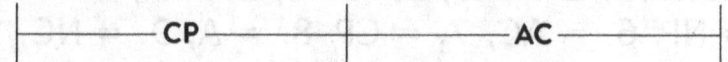

"If you don't do what's right, I have ways to get you to do it."

"It's your fault I had an affair because you didn't care about my feelings."

Critical Parent/Natural Child

"Mow that lawn perfectly. But stay away from where I'm getting a tan."

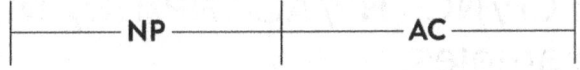
"I'm off to the pool. Get that homework done correctly."

Nurturing Parent/Adaptive Child

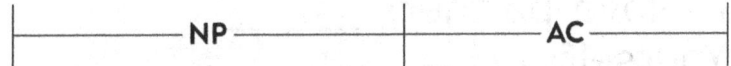
"I help you all the time. Why can't you help me?"

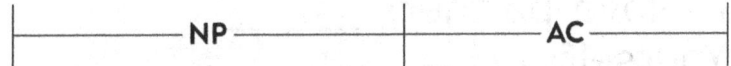
"I'm glad you like what I gave you. Now, where's my present?"

Nurturing Parent/Natural Child

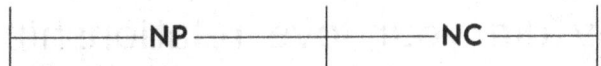
"I'll do whatever you need. Please don't leave me."

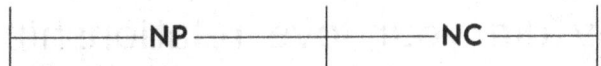
"I'm happy when you're happy. Let's be happy forever!"

Natural Child/Adaptive Child

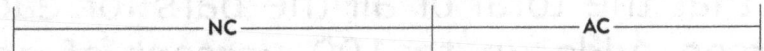
"Couldn't help myself. No payments for a full year! I've been waiting three months for this."

|———AC———|———NC———|

"It's too hot to pull weeds. I'll play tennis instead."

Which ego-state combination voices did you hear from the following (NP/CP, CP/AC, CP/NC, NP/AC, NP/NC, NC/AC)? Give examples.
Mother: _____
Father: _____
Ex-love-partner: _____
Yourself: _____

Revealing Your Relationship Patterns

Why did your love relationship end? Get a good idea by filling out the ego-bars, one set for you and one set for your ex-partner. Base this on relationship behaviors during the most difficult period of time when both of you were still committed. This will reveal the polarized patterns that most likely contributed to divorce. Rate each bar so that the total of all the bars for each person adds up to 100 percent of one bar.

	0%	50%	100%
Critical Parent			
Nurturing Parent			
Adult			
Adaptive Child			
Natural Child			

Ego-Bars for Yourself

	0%	50%	100%
Critical Parent			
Nurturing Parent			
Adult			
Adaptive Child			
Natural Child			

Ego-Bars for Your Ex-Partner

What did you find? _____

The overwhelming majority of seminar participants discovered they were in a parent-child, over-responsible–under-responsible relationship where one partner was mostly in one or both parent ego states and the other partner was mainly in one or both child ego states. Many people realized they switched ego states, sometimes being in the parent and at other times in the child. Ask yourself: How much of each person was in the healthier adult ego state? (Adult-centered partners can also grow apart, but their divorce tends to be more amicable due to the maturity of their personalities.)

Parent-child, or over-responsible–under-responsible, is a fundamental pattern behind unhealthy and unhappy relationships where neither partner accesses all three ego states, each relying on the other to complete relationship tasks. This means that one partner does the over-responsible "thinking-and-doing work" of the parent and detached adult while the other partner does the under-responsible "feeling-and-fun stuff" of the child. Often, such agreements are made unconsciously and duplicate roles from one's family of origin. (As someone once said, "We become like one parent and marry the other.")

If one partner changes by making healthier choices, the other person is threatened as these unspoken agreements are endangered. They could stay together only if both partners either return to unhealthy patterns or evolve the relationship by connecting to their detached ego state(s) while strengthening their adult. This is possible, though difficult. If only one partner changes, the relationship cannot continue. Perhaps this is why your love relationship ended.

After divorce, an unrecovered child may likely seek another over-responsible parent to take care of him or her. An unrecovered parent may likely find another child to care for. However, by decoding the patterns in your ended relationship, you'll be able to see your part and change to access all three ego states appropriately from an adult-centered perspective. This will help you avoid unhealthy partners and find the positive relationship you deserve.

Balance Yourself to Create Healthier Relationships

To become a balanced adult requires different tasks depending in which ego state(s) you're stuck (according to the ego-bars). In the following section, find what matches your ego state(s) and complete the short exercises. Then, jot down your emotional reaction to each one. If you're not sure what you are, do them all. As you read through them, pay particular attention to the exercises that evoke a strong negative reaction because this likely means the activity challenges ingrained unhealthy behavior patterns.

Natural Child and Adaptive Child
Both of these ego states have under-responsible behavior. The natural child lets things go; the adaptive child manipulates to get another to be responsible. Balance occurs when each take on appropriate responsibility.

1. *Natural child:* Be responsible and make that bed, do those dishes, complete that chore.
Emotional reaction: _____
2. *Adaptive child:* Be responsible and stop trying to get someone else to do your work for you, for example, don't feign busyness or give excuses, do the dishes, make your bed, or finish that chore.
Emotional reaction: _____

"Recovering" child-types report greater satisfaction with their lives. They are more organized, get things done, and find life less confusing. This leaves them with time to have fun sensibly. In other words:

Adaptive Behavior	to	Authentic Behavior
Needy and hurt child		Natural and creative child
Mimics others		Creative and spontaneous
Concerned about fitting in		Inner directed
Prompts rescuing from others		Prompts spontaneity in others
Rebel		Healthy identity
Upsets system		Helps system work better
Behavior results in more chaos		Behavior results in efficiency and effectiveness
Selfish manipulation		Positive persuasion

Critical Parent

These exercises will help you recapture the spontaneous joy of childhood by letting go of the compulsion to be an over-responsible perfectionist or living always in your head.

1. *Let something go this week.* Make it simple (don't endanger your job). Dr. Bruce Fisher liked to ask critical parents to stop making their bed for a week. Or, let go of something else that you must have "just so." (Cheryl let go of criticizing her children. She was amazed how much better they behaved!)

    Emotional reaction: _____

2. *Have some fun.* Moesha went to the park and hopped on the swings. At first, she felt self-conscious. Then, the joy of once-forgotten childhood summers returned.

    Emotional reaction: _____

3. *Keep a log of your emotions.* When something happens this week, write down your feelings, for example when receiving a gift,

getting cut off in traffic, being asked a favor, or forgetting something.

Emotional reaction: _____

"Recovering" critical parents are overjoyed to find peace and relaxation. They also relearn when it's appropriate to be exacting and when to "let it all hang out." Go from adaptive behavior to authentic behavior:

Adaptive Behavior	to	Authentic Behavior
Perfectionist		Strives for excellence
Expect perfection in others		Gives constructive feedback to others
Provides rigid limits		Provides healthy limits
Wants to change others		Accepts others
Rational and logical		Thoughts and feelings balanced
Rigid		Flexible
Concerned about doing it the right way		Concerned with what works for self and others
Forces opinions to convince others		Expresses beliefs and listens to others

Nurturing Parent

If you are over-responsible as a "good giver" (people-pleaser) and a "poor taker" or one who may give to receive yet deep down questions self-worth, do the following:
1. Ask someone to nurture you and only say, "Thank you." Do nothing for them in return.

Emotional reaction: _____
2. Say no to someone's request for assistance (especially if you realize deep down that you don't want to do it).
Emotional reaction: _____
3. Nurture yourself. Go have fun!
Emotional reaction: _____

"Recovering" nurturing parents find it liberating to ask for their needs to be met and feel life as more full, exciting, and less tiring. If this is you, let your motto be: *do unto yourself as you would do unto others.* Change from adaptive to authentic:

Adaptive Behavior	to	Authentic Behavior
Over-responsible		Responsible for self
Smothers		Empathic nurturing
Giving is self-serving		Gives with needs of self and others in mind
Caretaker		Caregiver
Feels selfish caring for self		Enjoys self-care

Detached Adult

Detached adults live disconnected to either the parent or the child, going through life like a robot, striving to live without ups and downs. Reconnect to the detached parts.

1. *Adult detached from critical parent:* Explore a given task by following specific instructions instead of trying to do it without guidance.
   Emotional reaction: _____
2. *Adult detached from nurturing parent:* Practice giving to others (a flower, back rub), asking and receiving from others (a favor, back rub, help with a chore), and giving to yourself (buying an inspirational book, enjoying a hobby).
   Emotional reaction: _____
3. *Adult detached from adaptive child:* Look for creative solutions to tasks.
4. *Adult detached from natural child:* Take a small notebook and jot down your feelings several times throughout the day. Take time to do "silly" activities, like fly a kite, go to a garage sale and wander around, or go for a stroll to nowhere in particular.
   Emotional reaction: _____

Remember, you maintain balance when you listen to all of your thoughts, feelings, wants, and desires. The balanced adult connected to all parts of the self is the best judge of what's appropriate. It helps you meet your needs with others and with yourself. Use the Healthy Adult visualization (download from http://www.newharbinger.com/45397) to bring you to an experience of your balanced self.

Will's Take *"If you do what you've always done, you'll get what you've always gotten." Therefore, if you don't balance yourself using an adult-centered perspective, names and faces may change, but your relationship(s) will remain the same. Hopefully, this thought will be scary enough for you to become dedicated to growth.*

As you continue your climb up the rebuilding blocks, your commitment to heal will be needed as denial gets replaced by the emotions of abandonment and loss. The next chapter will begin guiding you through these feelings.

Journaling to Freedom

Write a letter from your adult self to your child and parent selves. State your intentions to listen and learn from them as your adult self decides what's best.

Dear Child and Parent Selves,

_____
_____
_____
_____
_____
_____
_____

Actions Steps for Moving Onward

Do these tasks and share the results with a trusted friend or support group.

1. Answer the questions on which ego-state voices you heard from mother, father, ex-love-partner, and yourself.

2. Take the ego-state identification quiz.

3. Do the ego-bar assessments of you and your ex-partner.

4. Choose an activity to balance your ego states and note your emotional responses.

5. Listen to the Healthy Adult visualization (downloadable audio) at least three times this week.

6. Write a letter from your adult self to the other ego states.

7. Celebrate your efforts through healthy nurturing: eat a fine meal, see a movie with a friend, or go for a swim.

Chapter 5

Overcoming Loneliness

Loneliness is a word to express the pain of being alone. Solitude is a word to express the glory of being alone.
—Paul Tillich

STEPS ALONG THE WAY

1. **Understand Your Loneliness: What Are the Unmet Needs?**
2. **Loneliness as Relationship Hunger**
3. **The Process to Overcome Loneliness**
4. **Building a Support Network**

Loneliness may appear as the darkest corner of abandonment. It's no wonder some people seek any relationship to ease this pain. Yet, love partners chosen for this reason are notoriously incompatible and often create greater loneliness when that relationship ends. The problem is not the emotion of loneliness. It's the meaning you give to its experience and the choices you make to deal with it. The way through will become clear when you learn what loneliness has to teach you about yourself.

Understand Your Loneliness

Emotions indicate needs. Anger lets us know we want change or protection. Grief reveals the need for solace. Happiness reflects the desire for pleasure. Loneliness is a special, poignant emotion because it points you inward and outward at the same time. It shows a need to relate: with yourself, with others, and with life itself. Clark E. Moustakas (1972, 22) expressed this well. He wrote, "Being alone is a way back to others. Being lonely is a way back to oneself."

The first step to overcome loneliness is to fully understand your experience of it. This examination holds great opportunities for growth. Listen to the Loneliness Exploration visualization downloadable audio, available at http://www.newharbinger.com/45397. What does your loneliness say to you? Determine how and in what ways you experience loneliness. Be as specific as possible.

Loneliness Assessment

To me, loneliness is: _____

When lonely, I also feel: _____

I'm most likely to feel lonely when: _____

When feeling lonely, I (behavior): _____

Loneliness leaves me when: _____

Rebuilding Seminar participants generally agreed about loneliness:
- It stems from being without companionship.
- Often, it sparks fear that the isolation will last forever.

- It can strike at any time, whether by oneself or with others.
- For some, the greatest loneliness occurred when feeling alienated from other members of a group.
- It often hit during nighttime and weekends when not in a regular routine.

Okay, what can be done about it? First, let's figure out what you feel lonely about and then look at how you try to deal with it. Which relationship-loss situations bring up the deepest feelings of loneliness?

Loneliness-Situation Checklist

Rate each item on a scale of 1 (low) to 10 (high) in terms of how deeply you experience loneliness. Add others that may affect you.

Loss of:	Rating 1-10
1. Love partner	
2. Companionship	
3. Self-esteem	
4. Child(ren)	
5. Free time (as single parent)	
6. Friends	
7. Family support	
8. Possessions	
9. Financial resources	
10. Pets	
11. Dreams for the future	
12. Simplicity (life is now more complicated)	
13.	
14.	
15.	

Which three were your highest? _____

Your reaction: _____

Loneliness as "Relationship Hunger"

Betsy Callahan (1979) gave a classic definition of loneliness as "relationship hunger," which leads toward greater understanding of self and a plan of action that will help you meet your underlying needs.

Society places a high value on both individuality and coupleship. This puts us between two conflicting needs: standing apart to proclaim our uniqueness and engaging in satisfying relationships. To be out of touch with oneself or to be without connection to another creates this "relationship hunger" from which we can feel alienated, lonely, and unworthy.

We desire many different kinds of food to satisfy our physical hunger. Similarly, we have different relationship needs at the core of relationship hunger. To satisfy your hunger to relate, whether by caring for yourself or by connecting with others, first recognize your underlying psychological needs.

Psychological Needs

Abraham Maslow (2013) is perhaps the most famous of those proposing psychological needs. There is a wide range of thought on these, some extensive, others more compact. Richard

Ryan and Edward Deci (2018) have filtered them into three basic categories: relatedness, autonomy, and competence. The following breaks down those categories into needs most applicable to the divorce-recovery process.

Relatedness Needs
- *Relationship:* To belong with a significant other(s) in meaningful ways prompts bonding between lovers, family members, and friends.
- *Touching and holding:* Satisfies the "skin hunger" of physical intimacy. Sexual expression is only one aspect.
- *Nurture:* The desire to give and to receive.
- *Identification:* To experience togetherness by identifying with another. Examples: the adolescent who watches a parent learns how to act as a "man" or "woman," the adult who seeks out a career mentor.

Autonomy Needs
- *Differentiation:* To be uniquely oneself. This occurs when a person

desires a career different from the family business.
- *Personal power:* To make choices in behavior or environment and have others respect them, for example the adult who moves away from the hometown.

Competency Needs
- *Affirmation:* To be admired as a unique individual. Examples: the child who delights in seeing parents post a positive report card, the adult who enjoys compliments at work.

Unmet needs underlie loneliness and can contribute to the ending of a love relationship. For example, one may leave due to an unfulfilled need for differentiation caused by a smothering love partner. Or, an individual felt unloved because the need for affirmation went unmet. When a love partner leaves, the remaining partner's loneliness can come from several unmet needs: the need for relationship, the need for touching or holding, and the need to nurture.

People feel loneliness when they fail to meet these underlying needs and try to avoid the emotion through unhealthy behaviors. For example, the divorced person who attempts to satisfy companionship needs by having a one-night stand only intensifies loneliness the next morning. Those who try to escape loneliness through constant activity feel lonelier when they return to empty homes at the end of the day.

Feeling lonely is not the problem. It's what you do when it occurs. There are various styles where people perpetuate loneliness through ineffective behaviors (Callahan 1979, 83–87; Limón and Whalen 1986, 107–109). Here's a concise summary:

1. Forces relationship
    a. *Smotherer* demands so much time and attention that others leave.
    b. *Anyone will do* chooses unsuitable partners; relationships end.
2. Rejects relationship
    a. *Critical parent* can't find the "perfect" person.

    b. *Busyholic* is too busy with activities or work.
    c. *Pain avoider* won't risk, fears getting hurt.
    d. *Phantom* hides through humor or other means.
    e. *Self-sufficient* isolates and increases loneliness.
    f. *Alone in my own world* stays stuck in fantasy (through drugs, alcohol, eating, internet, TV).
3. Combination
    a. *The controller* invites relationship, then stifles it through demands.
    b. The *sex fiend's* demands for physical intimacy sabotage deeper intellectual or emotional connection.
    c. *Close, but not too close* wants love but afraid true intimacy will substantiate suspected unworthiness.
Can you add other styles? _____
_____

Consider these two examples of ineffective behaviors and how they foster loneliness.

1. Judy's fear: Loss of having any love partner.

    Ineffective behavior style: Busyholic.

    Behavior: Whenever I feel lonely about not being in a relationship, I clean up the house, work in the yard, even work overtime, anything to avoid these feelings.

    Result: Time goes by, but I don't think I'll ever stop feeling lonely. I don't have time to connect with others because I'm too busy.

2. Ben's fear: Loss of possessions and financial resources

    Ineffective behavior style: Alone in my own world.

    Behavior: When I feel lonely about losing money, the house I lived in, and the car I used to drive, I just go to a bar and drink.

    Result: I spend too much money on liquor, and I'm beginning to have health issues and problems at work.

Examine how your behavior may contribute to your pain. Do this by choosing your top three losses from the Loneliness-Situation Checklist. Relate your behavior using any ineffective style in the same manner as in the foregoing examples.

Loneliness-Behavior Assessment

1. Loss of: _____
Ineffective behavior style: _____
Behavior: _____

Result: _____

2. Loss of: _____
Ineffective behavior style: _____
Behavior: _____

Result: _____

3. Loss of: _____
Ineffective behavior style: _____
Behavior: _____

Result: _____

What I learned from this: _____

The Process to Overcome Loneliness

You learn most from loneliness when you embrace its experience, understand its message, and act to meet the underlying need. Running away from the feeling only causes it to increase in intensity. The sooner you accept loneliness, the more quickly you'll find peace. There are three steps in this process:
1. Experience your loneliness.
2. Change your loneliness to aloneness.
3. Develop all-wholeness.

1. Experience Your Loneliness

Instead of running away from lonely feelings, take the time to fully experience them. Sit or lie down. Hug yourself. Breathe deeply and let the emotion flow through you. Remind yourself that these feelings are inside you; they are *not* who you are. You are a unique human being worthy of love and admiration.

Confirm your ability to care for yourself. Also, believe in your ability to find the nurturing you need from those around you. Listen to the Embracing Loneliness visualization (available for download at http://www.newharbinger.com/45397) to help you.

Healthy ways I can feel my loneliness:

1. _____
2. _____
3. _____

There is no greater strength than the capacity to be present and loving in your relationship with yourself. As Charles C. Colton reportedly wrote: "To dare to live alone is the rarest courage since there are many who had rather meet their bitterest enemy in the field, than their own hearts in their closet."

Will's Take *I remember one evening after my divorce when I paced back and forth in my small apartment, saying to myself, "I'm lonely, I'm lonely, I'm lonely." Eventually, I became aware of someone talking: me. I had been* *trying to get involved with somebody else and had forgotten about me. It wasn't until I began to relate to myself that I started to get over my loneliness.*

2. Change Your Loneliness to Aloneness

Aloneness is an affirmation that you understand your needs and can care for yourself. It's a time of self-reflection where you build a better relationship with yourself prior to relating with others.

Develop solitude in your aloneness. *Learn to define times alone as being with someone you love: yourself!* Engage in nourishing activities, such as music, reading, walking, or hiking. Avoid harmful, mood-altering behaviors like overeating, oversleeping, drinking alcohol, or spending excessive amounts of time watching TV or online shopping or surfing. Appropriate physical activity is wonderful because it increases good health and lifts your spirits by releasing endorphins, the body's natural painkillers.

Consciously care for yourself. Understand when you're likely to feel lonely. Educate yourself about your particular wants and needs, and have activities available to address them. Examples are in parentheses.

When You Feel Lonely	What Can Be Done
(When I go to bed.)	Read an inspirational book.)
(On the weekends.)	Take a walk in the neighborhood.)

Will's Take *That experience of saying "I'm lonely" over and over helped me go from loneliness to aloneness where I developed pursuits that I enjoyed doing by myself. I'd go up into the mountains alone to play my French horn to hear it echo. Also, I started going to movies by myself. At first, I felt self-conscious. Then, I found that I really enjoyed it. There wasn't anyone to argue with me about what it meant; I could enjoy that too!*

3. Develop "All-Wholeness"

When your aloneness helps you become firmly rooted in yourself, relationships with others grow healthier. This is the "all-wholeness" stage. Here, you have the knowledge and the freedom to connect with others without being needy. You're more able to give and receive positive nurturing.

Take the following assessment to help you identify and evaluate particular wants you may have with others. Add additional ones that occur to you.

Relating-Desires Assessment

Rate each relationship desire. Add others as you can. Scale: 1 (low desire) to 10 (high desire).

1. Be adventurous
2. Help me when I'm ill
3. Career companion
4. Be athletic
5. Express spirituality
6. Be fun
7. Provide companionship
8. Be a "roomie"
9. Help me grow as a person
10. Support me when I'm feeling down
11. Do things
12. Cuddle (without sex)
13. Go "retailing"
14. Challenge my brain
15. Parenting support
16. Cheer me on
17. Teach me
18. Share meals
19. Share affection and loving
20. Receive compliments
21. Express emotions
22. Give compliments
23. Enjoy sexual intimacy
24. Assist me
25. Explore natural world
26. Decision-making support
27.
28.
29.
30.

Connect with others to receive support and to be supportive. Volunteer. This can help put your difficulties into perspective as well as build bridges beyond the transition of divorce. Meet those with whom you have similar interests and careers.

Will's Take *When aloneness helped me find all-wholeness, I found myself participating in all kinds of relationships: family member, friend, coworker, date, and love partner. I also discovered that I could relate well with just one other person, several people, or in a large group. By overcoming loneliness from the inside out, I realized that my well-being is based on the positive relationship with me. Others add to this happiness. As a friend told me, "Happiness is an inside job."*

Building a Support Network

First, keep track of individuals and groups that help meet your needs: list the person or group, the need met, the activity that meets the need, and ways to contact these individual(s). Be careful to manage your support system by replacing anyone who no longer meets a need or who is no longer available.

Make this list of contacts when you feel positive. If you do it while feeling lonely, you may not be able to think of anyone and that would defeat the purpose. Keep the list handy for when you have needs and don't know who to turn to. Add more as you can. These people are invaluable!

Individuals

1. Name: _____
Contact information: _____
Need(s) met: _____
Activity (activities) that meets need(s): _____

2. Name: _____
Contact information: _____
Need(s) met: _____
Activity (activities) that meets need(s): _____

3. Name: _____
Contact information: _____
Need(s) met: _____
Activity (activities) that meets need(s): _____

4. Name: _____
   Contact information: _____
   Need(s) met: _____
   Activity (activities) that meets need(s): _____

Groups
1. Name: _____
   Contact information: _____
   Need(s) met: _____
   Activity (activities) that meets need(s): _____

2. Name: _____
   Contact information: _____
   Need(s) met: _____
   Activity (activities) that meets need(s): _____

3. Name: _____
   Contact information: _____
   Need(s) met: _____
   Activity (activities) that meets need(s): _____

Here are some important ingredients for group interactions:
- A caring connection
- Each person responsible to communicate needs
- Mutual decisions on behavior and boundaries, for example, hugs are okay but sexual advances aren't
- Evaluate actions and make changes
- Make clear how members can respectfully end involvement

This clarity can forestall common pitfalls: empty promises, abrupt terminations, and unclear needs and expectations. This type of group interaction is useful for meeting social needs and getting emotional support. It's also excellent for building friendships with both sexes, the healthiest starting point for newly single individuals.

Make Specific Plans to Meet Loneliness Needs

Using the suggestions and resources in this section, choose one of the three items you evaluated in your Loneliness-Behavior Assessment. Determine the underlying need(s) and brainstorm achievable goals to help meet the need(s) in healthy ways. Then, set steps for carrying out your plan as well as a specific timeframe in which to accomplish your goals. (Look at the guidelines in chapter 3 on how to choose a plan of action, step 3 of the framework for conquering fear.) Specificity is important for success. Remember, you are responsible for getting your needs met. And, as you act, new people and situations will enter your life. You'll be excited at how living will be more enjoyable. When ready, do more. The following examples can guide you.

Loneliness Situation: Loss of Love Partner

Need(s): To nurture, to relate and belong, for touching and holding.

Goal(s): Join a volunteer organization working with under-served children, my child's school, or a church group. Join a group of other adults working through divorce-recovery issues.

Plan:
1. Call city and county agencies to inquire about public and private organizations that need volunteers.
   Do this by: Friday of this week.

2. Call my child's school and ask about volunteer opportunities.
   Do this by: Tomorrow.
3. Ask friends, a counselor, look on the internet (for example http://www.rebuilding.org) to find a divorce-recovery group.
   Do this by: One week from today.

Loneliness Situation: Loss of Free Time (Becoming a Single Parent)

Need(s): For personal power (choice), nurture (get support).

Goal(s): Join Parents Without Partners. Get involved in a babysitting co-op.

Plan:
1. Search the internet to find Parents Without Partners contacts.
   Do this by: End of this week.
2. Contact PWP organization, inquire about next meeting.
   Do this by: One day after obtaining contact info.
3. Attend PWP meeting.
   Do this by: Whenever next meeting occurs.

4. Talk to other parents in the neighborhood about babysitting co-op.
Do this by: The end of this weekend.

Plan for Meeting Loneliness Needs

Loneliness situation: Loss of: _____

Need(s): _____

Goal(s): _____

Plan: _____
1. _____
Do this by: _____
2. _____
Do this by: _____
3. _____
Do this by: _____
4. _____
Do this by: _____

Journaling to Freedom

Write a statement that connects with your deepest self and uses solitude to bring a greater awareness of your needs. Commit to meeting these needs with healthy others.

_____
_____
_____
_____
_____
_____
_____

As you move beyond the rebuilding block of loneliness, you naturally begin working on healing woundedness. You'll start by dealing with feeling "damaged" (unlovable, guilt, and rejection), then heal grief and work through anger.

Action Steps for Moving Onward

1. Complete the exercises in this chapter and share with trusted friends.
    a. Loneliness Assessment
    b. Loneliness-Situation Checklist
    c. Loneliness-Behavior Assessment
    d. Relating-Desires Assessment

2. Discuss with a trusted friend the ways individuals perpetuate loneliness.

3. Listen to the Loneliness Exploration and Embracing Loneliness visualizations (downloadable audio files).

4. Listen to the Being Alone meditation (downloadable audio).

5. Determine healthy ways to act when feeling lonely.

6. Choose three wants from the Relating-Desires Assessment and actively seek to meet them with healthy friends.

7. Begin to fill out your support network contacts for individuals and groups.

8. Determine a major need underneath your feelings of loneliness and carry out your plan to meet it using the Plan for Meeting Loneliness Needs.

9. Write your statement of connectedness to your deepest self.

10. Recognize your growing ability to overcome your loneliness by nurturing yourself—take a refreshing

walk or bike ride, listen to favorite music, have coffee with a friend.

Part II

Healing Woundedness

Feeling wounded may seem permanent. Yet, when you identify and experience the emotions of woundedness, you not only heal, you also gain valuable skills that bring new energy and self-empowerment. These chapters will lead you there.

Chapter 6 defines feeling "damaged" at the core of woundedness. You'll explore underlying emotions that begin repair and gain an important awareness of the divorce process.

Chapter 7 encourages you to experience the relief that grieving brings.

Chapter 8 will help you begin to build the energy you need to move into your future through releasing anger about the past.

Chapter 6

"Damage" Control: Unlovable, Guilt, and Rejection

Sometimes I go about pitying myself, and all the time I am being carried on great winds across the sky.
—Ojibway proverb

STEPS ALONG THE WAY

1. **Feeling "Damaged" Beyond Repair and Becoming "Love-able" for Yourself**
2. **Guilt and Rejection: Dumpers vs. Dumpees**
3. **Healthy Guilt**

Do you feel damaged as if you had "Divorce" written across your forehead? When your love relationship ends, this response is common. *Though you may not believe it, this feeling won't last forever.* This chapter will help you get beyond feeling damaged by exploring the underlying emotions—unlovable, guilt, and rejection—and show how they can foster healing by teaching powerful lessons.

Feeling "Damaged" Beyond Repair

The emotion of *unlovable* is a major part of feeling damaged from divorce. You may even feel it as, "I'm not able to love. I don't know how." Dwelling on this can lead to depression and despair, but another path is available. By deepening the relationship with yourself, you can work through feeling damaged and learn to love yourself and ultimately, feel worthy of being loved by others.

Love is an infinite, universal energy. It's what we strive for in relationship. However, as with loneliness, too many people think of love only in terms of a relationship with another and forget about the relationship with oneself. Even when connected with family, friends, or a love partner, the only guaranteed relationship is the one with yourself. To change un-love-ability into exchanging love with others, first learn to love yourself. Self-love acts as an antenna that receives the signals of love from others because as you love yourself, so you attract what is loving from another. Feel self-love during this time of change by nourishing yourself with what you want to give someone else. Like hugging yourself on a cold evening, turn your warmth toward yourself.

The Issue of Shame

For many, the deepest damage from divorce, and the one that diminishes self-love the most, is feeling shame. A child comes to feel shame about self when abandonment during childhood occurs through physical neglect and abuse, emotional condemnation, and intellectual ridicule. This causes the child to believe that he or she is fundamentally flawed as a person. A shame-based person perpetuates a poor self-image, low self-esteem, and unhealthy relationships because no positive alternatives were learned. Recognize shame for what it is: a lie. Being stuck in shame will slow down your progress toward divorce recovery just as it limits your joy.

Chapter 11, on self-worth, and chapter 13, on openness, delve more deeply into healing shame. For now, keep in mind that it's only through mistaken shame-based beliefs that you define your core self as unworthy. Your healing journey up the rebuilding blocks can help release you from the influence of lifelong shame. Realize that what has happened to you is *not* who you are. The mistakes you have made, including any issues about divorce, do *not* mean *you* are a mistake. Deal with errors in judgment through what is called "healthy guilt," which is discussed at the end of this chapter.

Becoming Lovable to Yourself

Let's begin experiencing self-love by looking again at the Relating-Desires Assessment in chapter 5. After reminding yourself of what you want from others, build on that self-loving connection by giving some of these things to yourself. Examples:
- Express emotions ... to yourself through journaling.

- Share affection and love ... with yourself by stroking your own face, saying loving words to yourself while looking in the mirror, giving yourself a warm hug.
- Express spiritually ... to yourself through meditation, walks in nature, spiritual reading.

Encourage yourself through notes and self-dialogs. These don't replace contact with others. These are ways of enriching the contact you have with yourself.

Look at the following categories and examples. Write down how you can increase your love for yourself.

Physical care (healthy eating, regular exercise): _____

_____
_____

Spiritual care (going to church, meditating each morning, keeping a journal): _____

_____
_____

Keep commitments to yourself (taking time off from work, going to a movie): _____

_____
_____

Engage in a hobby (knitting, crafts, gaming): _____

_____
_____

Physical pursuits (sports, biking, hiking): _____

_____
_____

Get yourself symbols of kindness (little gifts, books, flowers): _____

_____
_____

Will's Take Avoid "retail therapy"—spending money to distract from emotional pain. That doesn't work.

It only postpones your journey through the pain and adds more headaches financially. No one needs that.

When you demonstrate love for yourself, that can expand into a sense of unconditional love toward others. For example, you sit in a park and see people go by with their partners, children, or friends. You realize each of these individuals has his or her own drama unfolding as part of the wonderful variety of life. Because of your heartache, you feel greater empathy for them. As you relate from this deep respect, you do so without asking that they give back to you in return. Now, something amazing happens. Other people begin gravitating toward you. Chance meetings turn into meaningful interactions. A full sense of self-love will bring you this as it overflows to those around you.

Chapter 14, "Uncovering Self-Love," explores this in greater depth. Go to that chapter whenever you want to increase your love of self. For now, realize that life is a quest to experience all types of love. Your divorce journey can help you in this search. Commit to being with yourself just as you are and to share yourself with others just as they are, be they someone you meet on the street, a store clerk, a family member, friend, coworker, anyone. Love in your life is more than love for self or for one other person. It's more than just a one-to-one relationship. It's a one-to-all relationship. That's why there's more than one person on this planet.

Self-love will not only help you recover from feeling damaged, it will fortify you to deal with guilt and rejection as well.

Guilt and Rejection: Dumpers vs. Dumpees

When your love-relationship ends, there are any number of thoughts that can spark guilt: *I wish I hadn't done ... Maybe if I had said ... What if five years ago we had ...* These keep you caught in the "shoulda-coulda-wouldas." It's more important to put your energy into learning from what happened and start making better decisions. Since you can't change the past, living more effectively in the present is all you can do. Guilt is a choice. No matter what occurs, only you can make yourself feel guilty. Divorce will give you ample opportunity to confront this.

Rejection needs no introduction. Whether you're the one who walked away or the one who got left, you can feel rejected by everyone, even by life itself. If other significant losses or disappointments have occurred, such as career setbacks, financial difficulties, or illness or death of a child, divorce can be seen as the next installment in a pattern of rejection. This is dangerous because it may reinforce a low self-image and distract you from learning the lessons from this loss.

Except for those who mutually decide to divorce, usually one person initiates the ending, and the other must react to it. These roles are named "dumper" and "dumpee" (Fisher and Alberti 2016). Both have obvious differences in what they want for the relationship, and though they have the same healing journey, they begin it in different ways. Dumpers often talk like this: "I can't take it anymore. I've got to get out. I want to do my own thing. Good-bye." They usually experience more guilt than rejection because they feel responsible for their partner's pain. Dumpees typically talk like this: "Please, tell me what to change. I'll do anything, but I can't live without you." Dumpees usually feel more rejection than guilt when the love relationship ends.

Are You a Dumper, Dumpee, or Combination?

Discover where you fit.

Who initiated the ending of your relationship? _____

Why? _____

_____

When it became apparent your love relationship was going to end: _____

What did you say to your partner? _____

_____

What did you say about your partner to others? _____

_____

What did your partner say to you? _____

_____

What did you think about yourself? _____

How did you feel about yourself? _____

How did you feel about your ex-partner? _____

Many people think the divorce journey is different for men and women. That's not true. The major difference is this dumper-dumpee distinction. To become healthy, both must climb the rebuilding blocks to recovery. Typically, dumpers start their divorce process earlier than dumpees because they must move past denial to leave the relationship. Dumpees usually don't start until it's clear the relationship is ending. There's good news for dumpees however. Once they get through their denial, they tend to climb the rebuilding blocks more quickly because their pain is so motivating.

Most people going through divorce have elements of both the dumper and the dumpee. Determine what fits your situation from the following descriptions.

Responsible dumpers take ownership for their share of the problems in the relationship. They leave the relationship only after a great deal of inner struggle because they keep coming to the same conclusion: "This relationship is not going to work. It wouldn't be healthy for me, my partner, or our children if we stayed together."

Responsible dumpees are similar to responsible dumpers. They take responsibility for their part of the difficulties in the relationship, get counseling, and struggle with the issues. The difference between them is that responsible dumpees still want to work on the relationship.

Irresponsible dumpers tend to blame their partners: "It's all your fault. If you had only _____, things might've worked." Often, they waltz into another's arms without recognizing their role in bringing the end of the previous relationship. This can poison a new partnership. Until they take responsibility for their own stuff, irresponsible dumpers will tend to cocreate unhealthy relationships.

Irresponsible dumpees are similar to irresponsible dumpers, but they display it differently. In their conscious or unconscious desire to have it end, they sabotage the relationship by making things so miserable that their partner files for divorce. Then, irresponsible dumpees tell others, "Poor me, I've been dumped." These individuals also stay stuck by not taking responsibility for their part and not learning the lessons from their ended relationships.

Look at what you wrote about yourself and your partner about the end of your relationship. How do you see your role in the divorce (responsible dumper, responsible dumpee, irresponsible dumper, or irresponsible dumpee)?
Why? _____

How do you see your ex-partner's role? Why? _____

What behavior do you need to take responsibility for that led to the end of the relationship? _____

_____

_____

Most divorced people have behaved in a mix of responsible and irresponsible ways and have some degree of guilt and rejection. Healing both emotions is grounded in your own personal growth. Determine your part in the relationship difficulties, make changes in yourself, and dedicate yourself to being responsible. Examples:

The responsible dumper realizes, "I'm doing the best I can, and my partner also has the same opportunity to grow and change. I need not feel so guilty."

The responsible dumpee learns to take care of self and discovers, "Hey, that's just one person who left my life, not everyone on the planet. My feelings of rejection tell me that perhaps I overinvested in this relationship." As this person begins to heal, she or he can say, "You know, I'm getting healthier. My ex-partner really missed out."

Will's Take *I've asked seminar participants, "How much energy did you put in your relationship?" Donna (who was a dumpee) replied, "I put in 100 percent." Then I asked, "How much did you leave for yourself?" Her answer? "Nothing." She gave too much to her partner and asked her partner to relate to someone who was not even relating to herself! Can you see how this would impoverish a relationship and create a situation that could lead to divorce?*

One way to stay stuck in guilt or rejection is to be over-responsible for the problems that led to divorce. It takes two to create and maintain a relationship, and both partners contribute to the difficulties and their resolution. If you find yourself lost in feelings of guilt and rejection, review the Comparison: Desired vs. Actual Intimacy exercise in chapter 2 to underscore that each of you had a role to play.

To release guilt and rejection, keep in mind these wise words from an anonymous author:

Love is a gift one person makes to another....
is well to remember ... that you have no inalienable
rights to another's continued affection and that you have no obligation of your own to always love someone you once loved.
Sometimes, if your own life is to add up, you must subtract yourself from someone else's life. This time comes, I think, whenever you find that the affection or love of someone else can be kept only at the cost of your "seIf." If you are on the receiving side of much criticism, if the other has nothing but dissatisfaction with you, if you have lost the sense that to be yourself is a good and decent thing...
if it is painful and joyless ... it is time to let the love go and save yourself.
You will find another love, but never another self.

There is one type of guilt that can help you release your concern over the mistakes of the past, healthy guilt.

Healthy Guilt

Everyone makes mistakes. They may be small ones, like choosing an unsatisfactory meal from a menu, or big ones, like marrying an incompatible partner. Ultimately, mistakes aren't the issue. Whether or not you learn from them is what matters. *Healthy guilt* is the basis for healthy conscience. It guides you to the awareness of what you've done that was inappropriate and helps you take responsibility, indicating to whom you need to make amends.

Reflect on the mistakes you made in your ended relationship, those things you wish you had done differently.

_____
_____
_____
_____

Brainstorm how you may make appropriate amends, if possible, without damaging you or the other person. Examples: apologizing, returning an item, repaying a sum of money, or simply committing to act differently.

At the very least, you can demonstrate your willingness for amends by changing your behavior in future relationships. Don't allow the hurt of those incidents to keep you from considering them. As someone once said, "Remember the lesson, but forget the experience."

By learning from your mistakes, you take charge of your life. Healthy guilt will help you navigate divorce issues with humility and integrity. When you consider the effects your behavior on others, you can make better decisions based on a clearer sense of what's appropriate.

Journaling to Freedom

Write a letter to yourself about your willingness to experience your emotions of unlovability, guilt, and rejection. State your determination to keep these feelings from defining your worth. Commit to yourself that you will overcome any obstacle to your healing and renewed sense of joy.

Dear Self,

_____
_____
_____
_____
_____
_____
_____

Your feelings of unlovability, guilt, and rejection won't vanish overnight. They dissipate while releasing the emotions of woundedness—grief and anger—which we'll examine in the next three chapters. For now, listen to the Freeing Yourself from Damage visualization, available at http://www.newharbinger.com/45397.

Action Steps for Moving Onward

As with all exercises, share them with a trusted friend or support group to help you process feelings, develop insight, and heal.

1. Explore the feelings discussed in this chapter.

    a. Unlovable: Reexamine the Relating-Desires Assessment in chapter 5 and find ways to satisfy your own needs. Write down ways you can be more loving to yourself.

    b. Guilt and rejection: Review the Comparison: Desired vs. Actual Intimacy exercise in chapter 2 to determine proper responsibility and lessen unwarranted guilt and rejection.

2. Answer the questions to determine whether you were a dumper or dumpee. Then, answer the questions to determine who might have been a "good-bad" dumper and dumpee.

3. Listen to the Freeing Yourself from Damage visualization (downloadable audio) at least three times this week.

4. Listen to the When I Feel Guilt meditation (downloadable audio).

5. Reflect on the mistakes you made in your ended relationship to let healthy guilt guide you. Brainstorm how, if appropriate, you can make amends.

6. Write the letter to yourself to release feelings of being damaged and commit to healing yourself.

7. Nurture yourself as a reward for your courage to understand and overcome painful emotions: listen to music, spend time with children or a pet, start a new hobby. You're a valuable person and deserve to treat yourself as one.

Chapter 7

Cleansing Through Grief

The deeper that sorrow carves into your being, the more joy you can contain.
—Kahlil Gibran

STEPS ALONG THE WAY

1. **Why You Grieve**
2. **How You Grieve**
3. **Blocks to Awareness and Expression of Grief**
4. **Release Pain Through Grief Management**

Relationship loss brings forth a number of emotions. For many, the deepest pain is sorrow—for lost love, changed family, shattered dreams, and uncertain future. The passing of time alone doesn't relieve this hurt. But actively grieving helps you heal and become healthier than before. You decide the length of your grief process.

Bottom line: It's not the hurt you feel; it's how you feel the hurt.

"Why Do I Feel Grief?"

Take a few moments and rate the following losses on a scale of 1 (low) to 10 (high) for how each may foster grief or sadness. Add others if you need to. (Note: As with all assessments in this workbook, this assessment is meant to help you see how these issues are finite, not as a list of what you should feel.)

Issue	Rating: 1–10
Loss of:	
Love partner	
Future plans	
Love relationship	
Role of husband or wife or lover	
Status of being a couple	
House, possessions	
Children (not having custody)	
Free time (by having sole custody)	
Children's grieving loss of parent	
Renewal of past pain	
Replay of childhood deprivations, unfulfilled emotional needs	

What are your top three issues?
_____
_____

Your reaction? _____
_____

Whatever losses stand out for you, an underlying cause is the loss of what's called the "ideal image."

Loss of Ideal Image

Grief from divorce has its roots in childhood where we began to construct an ideal image of a love partner. Television, books, magazines, movies, and the internet describe many characteristics of ideal men and women, lovers and spouses. Of course, the most dominant role models were our parents in how they related to each other and to us. From these influences, we build an image (mostly unconscious) of the ideal mate.

At the beginning of a love relationship, couples bond not only to the actual partner, they also blend that partner into the long-held ideal image. This bonding process not only attaches (realistically or unrealistically) one partner to the other, it also connects one's self-image to the relationship. It's very painful when this process is reversed during divorce. You not only lose actual physical and emotional connection and ideal-image fulfillment, you also lose who you were in the relationship. This is at the heart of your grief: all at once, you experience the loss of love, lover, family, and self.

To see how this applies to you, compare your ideal image with what you actually received from your ex-partner. List aspects of what you desire in a committed love relationship. Then, rate (1 low, 10 high) their importance and the overall satisfaction from this one person. A difference between importance and satisfaction indicates how you may have mistakenly assumed this ex-partner would fulfill your desires. Congruence in rating indicates that your desire was met. Both are areas where you can feel grief: not getting what you wanted and having but losing your desires.

Desired Aspect	Importance	Satisfaction
Physical attributes (appearance, hygiene)		
1.		
2.		
3.		
4.		
5.		
Mental attributes (intelligence, humor, integrity)		
1.		
2.		
3.		
4.		
5.		
Emotional attributes (in touch with feelings, shares emotions)		
1.		
2.		
3.		
4.		
5.		

In what ways might you have attached your well-being to having this relationship: financially, socially, sexually, and so on?

_____
_____
_____

What stands out here as your most significant losses? _____

_____

Any loss, whether from a particular issue or from your ideal image, can combine with the financial and legal difficulties of divorce to make grief seem overwhelming. Yet, awareness and appropriate expression of grief will carry you through.

"How Do I Feel Grief?"

While some individuals react to loss with tears, many people find their grief cloaked in other kinds of physical, behavioral, emotional, and mental symptoms.

Physical Symptoms

Your body has a wisdom of its own, and without knowing it, you may have been grieving for a long time. Rate these symptoms on a scale of 1 (low) to 10 (high).

	Rating: 1–10
Tightness in throat, difficulty swallowing	
No appetite: weight loss	
Increased appetite: weight gain	
Empty or restricted feeling in stomach	
Weakness, helplessness	
Impotence or lack of interest in sex	
Illness: headaches, colitis, arthritis, asthma	
Pain in heart	
Shortness of breath	

Which three are your highest? _____

Your reaction? _____

Will's Take *During separation, my heart area ached with grief. I breathed through the sensation until it eased. Then, my throat tightened up. I breathed through that until the tears flowed. After crying, I felt much lighter.*

Behavioral Symptoms

Here's another area where you may not even be aware that you're grieving. Evaluate the behavioral symptoms.

	Rating: 1–10
Verbal diarrhea: talking about feelings instead of expressing them	
Push-pull effect: pull others close, push them away, repeat	
Isolate yourself	
Not sleeping	
Sleep too much	
Drug use	
Alcohol use	
Eat too little	
Eat too much	
Sighing often	
Crying	

Which three are your highest? _____

Your reaction? _____

These symptoms of grief can seem to suck the life-force right out of you. However, it's not the emotion that's doing it. *It's your inability or unwillingness to go through the grief process that may be holding you back.*

Emotional Symptoms

Along with sadness, a number of other emotions accompany grief from divorce. It's important to work down to the deepest emotional levels to reach complete healing. The further down this list, the greater emotional impact.

	Rating: 1–10
Lack of contact with your emotions	
Feeling emotionally drained	
Rapid mood changes	
Feel emotionally out of control, unable to keep from crying	
Sadness	
Loneliness	
Depression	
Guilt	
Rejection	
Anger	
Fears	
Devastation	
Abandonment	

Which three are your highest? _____

Your reaction? _____

For some people, abandonment in divorce grief is reminiscent of the abandonment they experienced as a child. The lack of acceptance from parents or parenting figures may have been the major influence to seek a love relationship. When divorce occurs, this original abandonment resurfaces. While it may feel daunting to face the abandonment of childhood as well as that of divorce, it's a priceless opportunity for growth. The process through which you grieve your divorce can be a model to help you to heal from all loss and abandonment issues.

Mental Symptoms

What you think sparks the emotions you experience. See how many of these thoughts have generated feelings of grief.

Mental Symptoms	Rating: 1–10
Loss of reality	
Fantasizing: seeing or hearing ex-partner, feeling that a body part is missing, such as heart	
Lack of concentration	
Lack of interest in sex	
Self-criticism	
Suicidal thoughts	
Thoughts of going crazy	
Thoughts of inadequacy	
Everyone else but you is happy	

Which three are your highest?
_____

Your reaction? _____

Note how all of these different types of symptoms—physical, behavioral, emotional, mental—are linked. For example, you can't sleep, your mind races, and your emotions go into overdrive. The next day you're spacy from lack of sleep and exhausted from all that internal fussing. These affect concentration, diet, and mood.

You may be thinking: *Wow, that's a lot of grief symptoms.* Not all may apply to you. Use these assessments in two ways. First, recognize your patterns of grief, for example, more emotional than behavioral, and so forth. Second, return to them as you heal to assess how your grief symptoms have lessened.

Some Frank Words About the Issue of Suicide

Divorce hurts, I know. During this time, it's common for anyone to have suicidal thoughts. This can range from passive ones—*Maybe the ceiling will cave in,* or *Maybe my heart will stop beating, and all this pain will be over*—to more dangerous active planning or acting out. First things first. Are you feeling safe? If you can't clearly answer yes to that question, reach out for help today. There are many organizations that can help, including the National Suicide Prevention Lifeline at 1-800-273-8255. Supportive family and friends can be there for you. A therapist or other helping professional is only a phone call away. Be wary of social media. It can be supportive, but there are often negative elements as well.

Remember, divorce is an acute situational crisis, painful, but bound up with this particular loss. While thoughts and feelings akin to suicide are common reactions, planning and attempting suicide are relatively rare and must always be addressed immediately. Someone in this position is not the best judge of what to do.

While some people see suicide as the only way out of the pain, others imagine it as some sort of revenge. However, it's inevitable that suicide would have a profound effect on those who care most about you. The pain is deepest for family members and children. The anger and hurt of children whose parents have killed themselves leave a much deeper scar than divorce ever could. In addition, parents who end their own lives foster a life pattern of self-destructive behavior for their children, including at least a three times greater chance for suicide (Johns Hopkins 2010). As for revenge, I've heard it said that the best revenge is to live well. At first, perhaps you'll do it only to spite your ex-partner. Later, when you're happy, who cares what the other person thinks!

Right now, make a commitment to yourself, your loved ones, and friends that if you ever have serious thoughts of suicide, you'll talk to them, your therapist, or whomever you trust before you would ever act destructively. Get others' input and support to help you see how to move through your pain healthfully. If you find it difficult to make this commitment, as soon as possible speak with a therapist, minister, support group, or friend about this. Again, any serious suicidal thoughts only confirm that you are not the best judge of what to do with your life at this point in time. Though these thoughts may scare you or even provide some comfort, remember that divorce is not the end of the world. It's really a new beginning. Know that reaching out to others is the best way to get from the dark of this emotional night into the dawn of the next day. Keep in mind:

Suicide is a permanent solution to a temporary problem!

Will's Take *During a difficult time in my marriage, I was out jogging on the side of the road as cars whizzed by. I saw how easy it would be to end my agony just by shifting three feet over into the highway. The thought scared me. As fear crowded in with my pain, I realized both emotions were not me, just inside me. I am bigger than what I feel. This gave me hope. Relieved, I jogged home, knowing I wouldn't ever have such self-destructive thoughts again. And, I haven't.*

Working through the rebuilding block process in this book will help greatly reduce any suicidal thoughts and bring you to a place of hope and excitement about your future.

Behaviors That Block Awareness and Expression of Grief

Regardless of how grief affects us—physically, behaviorally, emotionally, or mentally—many individuals never learned how to grieve and find themselves out of touch with their emotions when faced with relationship loss. They often experience discomfort when others feel sorrow. This is particularly true of males.

Here are some typical barriers to awareness and expression of grief:

1. Well-meaning friends who tell you: "Stop moping. It's been a month since it ended. Go out, have fun, find somebody else." These people have either never experienced relationship loss or are uncomfortable because your pain brings up their unresolved grief.

2. Becoming one who either overworks or overplays to exhaustion.
3. Mood-altering compulsive behaviors: shopping 'til you drop, gambling, drinking, taking drugs, one-night stands, overeating, excessive TV watching or Internet surfing, or overexercising.

These avoidance behaviors prolong the pain of grief because they prevent you from feeling the emotion through. Also, they add new difficulties to life: financially, socially, and effects on your health. M. Scott Peck (1978) in his classic book *The Road Less Traveled* defined neurosis as the avoidance of legitimate suffering. No wonder people who distract themselves away from their feelings believe that they're "going crazy." Grief is a major part of the legitimate suffering during divorce. Don't be seduced into avoiding it or you will postpone your own healthy future.

What are ways you avoid grief?

1. _____
2. _____
3. _____
4. _____
5. _____
6. _____

Instead of avoiding, find the relief of release by consciously grieving through the pain of your loss.

Release Pain Through Grief Management

You manage grief by dwelling on objects that bring up pain to release your tears and hurt. When you do this in a private place, over time this desensitizes you to the loss. John spent a whole day looking at videotapes of the last ten family Christmases. He sobbed a great deal, but when he finished, he felt as if a great weight had been lifted off. You can do this by looking at your wedding album or pictures of your children or examining a meaningful souvenir. Express the sighs and tears that may arise. Manage your grief by setting an alarm for a half hour. Get into your sorrow during that time. When the alarm sounds, turn it off, wash your face, and walk around the house or yard for a while. Then, go back and do this again. This purposeful grieving will allow you to release the pain while managing the emotion. You'll see that the grieving process won't last forever. In desensitizing, you literally reclaim your life. Don't let a fear of grief hold you back; since grief is already here, use it to heal.

What items can you use for grief work?

1. _____
2. _____
3. _____
4. _____
5. _____
6. _____

Grief management helps you channel your emotion. Consider coworkers Joyce and Brenda, both of whom are getting divorced. Joyce manages grief by releasing it by herself and with close friends. Brenda holds in her sorrow. One day, someone tunes the radio to a particularly mournful song. Joyce hears the music, feels sad, and plans to take time to cry when she gets home. Brenda, however, cannot hold her tears back. They cascade down her cheeks as she tries to hide her face. She cannot stifle her grief any longer.

Here's how Liz tried to avoid grief. "I'll never go to our special restaurant again," she said. "I'll never talk to those friends again or go to that great hiking trail in the mountains ever, ever again." Tears welled up in her eyes. When she learned to manage her grief, she regained the enjoyment of those places and people she'd known in her relationship.

Studies have shown that tears contain different chemical enzymes for the different reasons why we cry. Whether peeling an onion, maintaining moisture in your eyes, or experiencing emotion, your tears are chemically different (Stromberg 2013). Stifling your tears may physically affect you. Some research indicates that crying leads to getting relief and uplifting mood (Gračanin et al. 2015).

Will's Take *I remember when my honeymoon picture that used to evoke* *hours of grief only brought forth a few minutes of tears. It's as if they'd all run out. I knew then my major grief work was ending.*

In preparation for the next section, listen to Grief Visualization, Part One, available at http://www.newharbinger.com/45397, to help you get in touch with your grief.

Journaling to Freedom

Write a letter of good-bye to your former love partner and whoever (or whatever) else brought up the most emotion for you in the visualization. **Do not send this letter** because your rapid growth will soon make this message obsolete. However, write it as if you were going to send it. Then, share it with a therapist, trusted friend, or family member who can give you support and help you grieve. Here are two examples:

From Sharon:

Good-bye to wonderful memories.
Good-bye to a bitter ending.
Good-bye to our morning showers—together.

Good-bye to filling our photo album with family pictures, of yours and mine.

Good-bye to feeling secure in the blanket of love.

Good-bye to the adventurous couple, partners, the team.

Good-bye to hearing "How's my babe?"

Good-bye to my once best friend.

Good-bye to the anger you have for me.

Good-bye to pain.

Good-bye to my hope for our future.

Good-bye to who I thought I was.

Good-bye to what once was. Today is today—and welcome future, with love!

From Kevin:

Dear Sheila,

This is a letter to you, but not for you. It's for me. It's just part of the work that I needed to do, so that I can get on with my life.

>*Good-bye.*
>*Good-bye to custody battle*
>*to frustration, wondering, waiting, never knowing*

to foolish wishes and dreams.

to a marriage that was destined to fail, even before it began

to the bitching when you couldn't get your way

to trying to please you, which is practically impossible

to being manipulated because I allowed myself to be

Good-bye feeling worthless, no matter what I did
to pouring my heart out to you and feeling like you just didn't care

to raising a family together

to your hugs, which I'd die for when I could get them

to growing old together

to hearing our kids saying "Mommy and Daddy" in one sentence

Good-bye to loving you—damn, that's hard to say!

I've got to go on now. I can't believe how hard this is, but in a way, it feels good to let go. I wish you the best with all my heart.

Now, from you:

Dear _____

_____
_____
_____
_____
_____
_____
_____

Nina Remembers... In Canada, a man shared his good-bye letter. As he read his eloquent words, tears flowed down his cheeks. Soon, all of us were in tears, each deeply touched by his incredible vulnerability.

This is my humble good-bye to my beloved husband Bruce.

For Bruce, my love,

A moment in time that is forever etched on my heart and in my soul.

My life changed in that one instant when you softly and tenderly died in my arms on that fateful
May afternoon.
My heart bursts with gratitude.
Thank you, my love, for sharing with me this very precious lifetime.
Thank you—for gently loving and trusting me.
for allowing me to cherish and nurture you in return.

for joyfully and boldly joining with me in the Mystery and the Magic.

for your open, willing commitment as my wise and clear Master Teacher.

for being Robert's father.

for always dancing with me to our heart's song.

Thank you, Bruce Franklin Fisher, for courageously giving me the greatest gift of my life.
I MISS YOU.

All I know NOW, in this moment, is that I will never be the same again.

You manage your grief to leave it behind. Listen to the Grief Visualization, Part Two (available at http://www.newharbinger.com/45397). Return to it to maintain this process in your mind and heart. Let it prepare you for this next letter, one to yourself.

Journaling to Freedom

Write a letter to you about your grief from the loss of your love relationship. Proclaim your sorrow and your willingness to feel it through until it's gone. Share your desire to support yourself and to have nurturing friends help you.

Dear Self,

_____

_____

_____

_____

_____

_____

Now is the time to take the love you might wish to give another and turn it back toward yourself. If you feel stuck, get individual therapy. Getting help is a sign of strength not weakness. The depth of your hurt is an eloquent testament to the love you sought in your relationship. This shows your willingness to risk vulnerability and your capacity to love another person. Working through grief will free you up for future joy.

For many, releasing grief opens the door to anger. We'll move on to this emotion in the next chapter.

Action Steps for Moving Onward

As always, discuss the results of your work in this chapter with a trusted friend or support group.

1. Assess why you feel grief.
2. Examine your ideal image and compare it with your ended relationship.
3. Assess how grief affects you:
   a. Physically
   b. Behaviorally
   c. Emotionally
   d. Mentally
4. Discuss your reactions to sorrow with family and friends; especially, share any self-destructive or suicidal thoughts. Make an agreement with them to reach out to others if any of these thoughts enter your mind.
5. List your blocks to awareness and expression of grief.
6. Select items for grief management. Practice grief management by taking quiet time to look at pictures or mementos or to listen to music. Share this time with a trusted, supportive friend.
7. Write a good-bye letter to your former love partner. It's important

that you share this with supportive others and grieve.

8. Write the letter to yourself about releasing grief.

9. If you have children, share, in age-appropriate ways, how grief can be expressed, and grieve together. As always, if you or your children are stuck, get professional help from a therapist or minister.

10. Contemplate Grief Visualization Parts One and Two (downloadable audio files) at least three times this next week. If you can, write new letters each time.

11. Listen to the To Feel My Sorrow meditation (downloadable audio).

12. Consciously nurture your body this week: take a hot bubble bath, get a massage, eat an especially nutritious meal.

13. Spend time planning a new future: Will you change careers or go back to school? Where do you want to be emotionally, psychologically, and physically two weeks from now, two months from now, and two years from

> now? Commit these goals to paper and begin to take specific steps to realize them.

Chapter 8

The Power of Anger, Part One: Releasing Anger About the Past

...and our very anger said a new "yes" to life.
—Betty Friedan

STEPS ALONG THE WAY

1. **Understanding Anger: The Anger Cycle**
2. **The Anger Process**
3. **Releasing Anger About the Past**
4. **Moving Toward the Future**

Anger is perhaps the most powerful of all emotions during divorce; it may last a lifetime. Yet, anger can also be an ally to motivate healthy change. The causes of anger are complex and easily misunderstood. We'll unpack these causes so you can realize why you get angry. Releasing anger about the past events requires a different response from coping with anger in current situations. Here, we'll examine the fundamentals of anger and focus on anger about the past, including activities to heal. The next chapter discusses dealing with anger in current situations.

Understanding Anger

Anger arises when you believe that another person, object, or situation is attacking or depriving you of something you want or need (Potter-Efron and Potter-Efron 2006). Anger's energy protects you from actual or perceived harm (McKay, Rogers, and McKay 2003). This seems simple enough, but you must know why you're angry to address both the emotion and the situation.

There's disagreement about whether anger is a primary emotion like grief, fear, and loneliness (Alberti and Emmons 2017) or a secondary emotion with underlying feelings that have different needs (Seltzer 2013). Nevertheless, since anger lets us know we believe we need protection or that we have needs not being met, let's explore what prompts anger and how our beliefs about those affect our experience.

Recipe for Anger

When baking a cake, it helps to follow a recipe. While anger may seem to arise instantly, there's a recipe for how it's generated. Cognitive behavioral therapy (CBT) decodes this process. Understanding this can lead to awareness, relief, and positive change. Let's examine the ingredients that go into anger: environmental, physical, psychological, and emotional.

Anger Ingredients

Environmental: Job stress, traffic jams, financial setbacks, family pressures all contribute to stress and anger (Alberti and Emmons 2017).

Physical:
- *Genetic.* Recent research indicates the "anger threshold" may be hardwired into our brain (Alberti and Emmons 2017).
- *Health.* Hunger, fatigue, and illness cause stress and susceptibility to anger triggers.

- *Substance abuse.* Drugs and alcohol reduce rational thought, affecting behavior.

Psychological:
- *Upbringing.* The way we're raised strongly influences how we interpret events and feelings and how we express emotions.
- *Attitudes and expectations.* Beliefs about whether or not we've been harmed and purposely victimized contribute to escalated anger (Davis, Eshelman, and McKay 2008). Life rules and attitudes about anger can contribute as well (Alberti and Emmons 2017).

Unmet needs, especially after expecting satisfaction, can bring anger (see chapter 5). Here are some of the unmet psychological needs:
- *Relatedness.* Relationship, touching and holding, nurture, identification
- *Autonomy.* Differentiation, personal power
- *Competency.* Affirmation

Emotional: Some theorists view anger as a secondary emotion because underlying feelings have their own needs. Here are four main emotions

under anger: frustration, hurt, fear or threat, inadequacy. Examples:
- My ex-partner won't reply to requests to get personal items. I was so *frustrated* I got really angry.
- Before divorce, my spouse cheated on me. I got angry because it *hurt* so much.
- My ex-partner brought our children home late without calling. I got angry because I was *fearful* something bad had happened.
- I asked my sister to watch my kids. She called me a bad parent for wanting alone time. I got angry because deep down I felt *inadequate*.

Your examples:
Frustration: _____

Hurt: _____

Fear or threat: _____

Inadequacy: _____

(Other emotion): _____

(Other emotion): _____

Nina Remembers... At a Chicago weekend workshop, a brilliant engineer shared about his anger process.

> I had grown up being out of control with anger, so I "stuffed" my feelings and lived in my head. Divorce was a catalyst for change. I learned to ask two questions when angry: What's happening that I don't want to happen? What's not happening that I want?
>
> These questions helped me drop deeper into the emotions I'd been running from—fear and hurt. Divorce pain turned out to be a gift of freedom—to be fully human and feel. I now like myself. For the first time, I want to be with my vulnerable, wounded parts. I'm growing. I'm healing. How fortunate I am!

With these ingredients, let's see how you "bake" your anger.

The Anger Cycle

Albert Ellis (1975) explained that our emotions are not generated from what happens to us but from the meaning (interpretation) we give to the experience:

Event → Interpretation → Emotion

With this as a foundation, CBT theorists often describe a cycle of how anger is kindled (Langelier and Connell 2005). The following image shows my interpretation of an anger cycle, starting with the event.

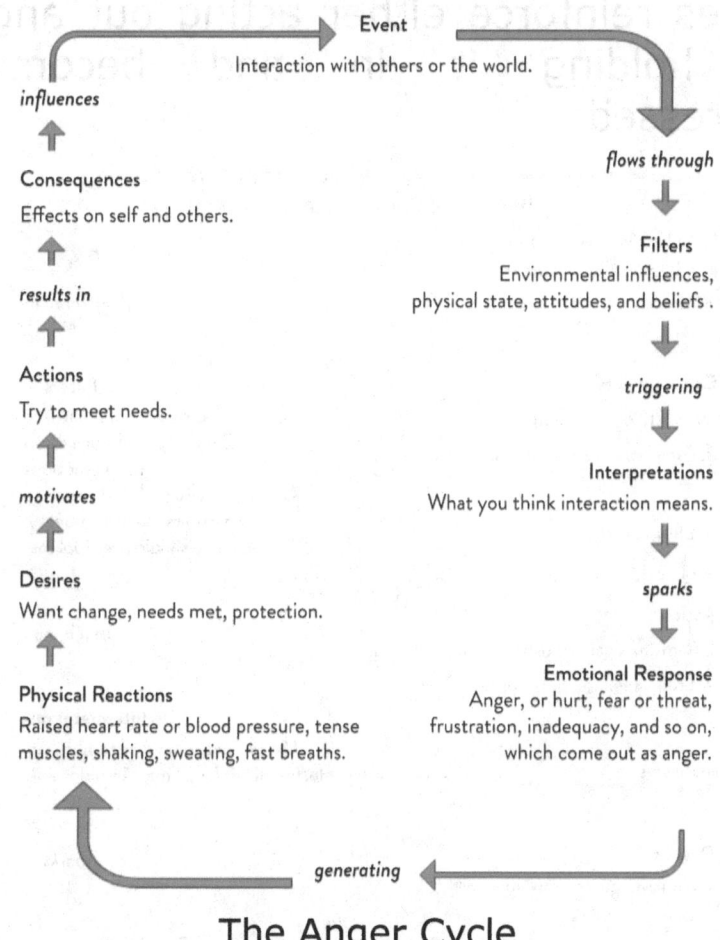

The Anger Cycle

Let's see how this would work for anger about the past using the previous example about the underlying emotion of hurt. While this is a past event, the rest of the cycle depicts current filters, interpretations, emotions, physical reactions, desires, actions, and consequences. Notice how the cycle becomes a negative spiral as repeated cycles reinforce either acting out anger or holding it in and becoming depressed:

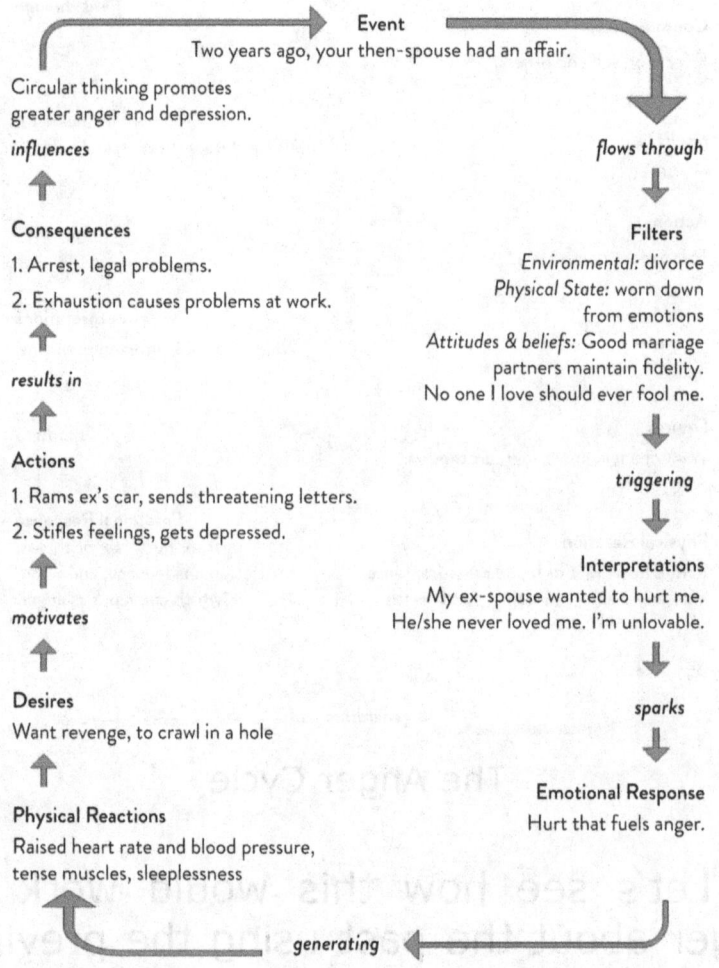

The Anger Cycle Example for Anger About the Past

See how filters and interpretations create the emotion?

Like grief, anger is not the problem. It's an indicator of your need to protect yourself. Difficulties arise when you either stifle your anger or express it destructively.

The Anger Process

As with grief management (discussed in chapter 7), anger has its own process of discovery and expression (Vilhauer 2015) that leads to your recovery from divorce. Here is a succinct four-step process on anger (Madow 1972) with my suggestions for dealing with anger about the past.

1. Recognize that you are angry.

    a. *Body cues.* Achy muscles without apparent cause, headaches, acidic stomach, and raised blood pressure can all indicate suppressed anger. Be aware of your body's reactions to internalized anger. Learn to address it before it causes physical illness.

    Your physical cues: _____

    b. *Words and phrases.* Saying you're irritated, annoyed, disappointed, or upset when, really, you're angry shows you're minimizing anger.

Your words when angry: _____

c. *Depression.* You feel depressed. You remember a friend sharing about a wonderful date. Now you're angry because your friend knows you're getting a divorce. Anger energizes you. The depression has gone away.

Ever felt depressed and found anger underneath? When?
_____
_____

2. Identify the source of your anger.

a. *Is it obvious or subtle?* Anger can be displaced. Christine's anger at her son had nothing to do with him; she was angry because the teen looked and acted like his father, her ex-husband. Before you express anger, know the cause. *If you have anger and don't know why, get professional assistance to help you discover its source.*

i. What are sources of your anger about the past? Which are apparent? Which may be displaced?

b. *Overreactions.* You explode suddenly and realize your anger doesn't fit the situation. Step back and determine the real source—possibly to avoid guilt or humiliation.

When you've overreacted, what's been the real source? _____

c. *Underreactions.* Sharing painful situations in a matter-of-fact tone is an underreaction attempting to avoid the anger and minimize the pain.

Describe when you've underreacted and your real feelings of anger: _____

There are multiple levels of anger awareness. The deeper you allow yourself to feel anger, the more you'll understand and use your anger effectively. Rate these emotions on a scale of 1 (low) to 10 (high) for how much you are aware of them and how often you express them. You can do this in terms of divorce issues or overall in your life. Rating both is important. They indicate patterns that have profound effects on your relationships because what you withhold from yourself tends to come out "sideways" toward others. What you withhold from others stresses the relationship in covert ways. The further down the list, the deeper the anger.

	Awareness	Expression
1. Judgmental		
2. Critical reactions		
3. Teasing behavior		
4. Sarcastic humor		
5. Annoyance		
6. Irritability		
7. Spite		
8. Rebelliousness		
9. Revenge		
10. Depression		
11. Anger		
12. Rage		
13. Abandonment		

What patterns do you see? (high awareness–high expression, high awareness–low expression, and so forth)

What are your top three in awareness? _____

What are the top three in awareness that are lowest in expression? _____

Your reaction: _____

3. Understand the basic reasons for anger. Anger is part of our

reaction when we don't get what we believe we should have. Anger about the past is often a reaction to when we felt frustration, hurt, fear or threat, and inadequacy and didn't realize we had those feelings or didn't express them.
4. Deal with the anger realistically. Realistic approaches to releasing anger about the past are different from expressing anger about current situations. The following section will help you.

Releasing Anger About the Past

The first step to resolving your divorce anger about the past is to get in touch with it. Listen to the Accessing Divorce Anger, Part One visualization, available at http://www.newharbinger.com/45397, to help you.

Journaling to Freedom

Write a letter to your former love partner or to any other person or object that brought out the most anger in the visualization. Proclaim your anger, release it, and give it back. **Do not send this letter because it could cause great difficulties legally and emotionally in your divorce process.** *Also, you are changing so rapidly, and it won't represent how you will feel in the future.* Note: Curse words are appropriate here. Don't let politeness prevent you from letting it all out. This is a good start toward releasing your anger and will prime the pump for the anger work in the second half of this chapter.

Dear (or not so dear) _____,

_____
_____
_____
_____
_____
_____
_____

Welcome to the "Bomb Squad"

Anger's explosive power can blow up in your face. Or, it can implode into depression and shame. If defused and rechanneled, anger energy can be a force for positive change. Like World War II bombs still being uncovered in Europe, anger about the past lingers, dangerous dynamite that can threaten your present and sabotage your future.

It takes a great deal of emotional energy to keep the lid on anger about the past, and if any new anger arrives, it's even more volatile. It does no good to blame others for these old hurts. What was said or done six months ago or six years ago cannot be changed. Release anger about the past appropriately. Like dealing with a bomb, there are two methods: defusing and safe explosion.

Defusing Anger from the Past

Go back to the anger cycle example where the spouse cheated during the marriage. There are multiple points in which you can practice defusing.

1. *Event.* Take the time to relax and get grounded in the now to remind yourself that is over and not in the present. Close your eyes; breathe deeply. Clear your

mind of thoughts and your body of feelings. Feel your feet on the ground and wiggle your toes to connect with the earth. Do this until you can actually feel the groundedness of here and now (Forsyth and Eifert 2016, 298).

2. *Filters.* Get better sleep and eat a healthier diet. Reexamine beliefs that set you up for anger, such as, "Good marriage partners maintain fidelity." If you change the belief that your ex-spouse was a "good partner," then what could you expect from such a person? The other belief, "No one I love should ever fool me," is unrealistic. We can't control others; we can only manage ourselves. Let go of this thought. That's practicing "stress inoculation," changing beliefs that set us up for stress and anger (McKay, Davis, and Fanning 2011.)

3. *Interpretations.* Practice coping thoughts that back away from blame and see things in a larger context, for example, "Blaming

keeps me stuck. I want to let go. His betrayal is his doing, and his future partners' problem, not mine anymore." Avoid anger distortions: blaming, magnifying, over-generalizing, mind-reading, and making general rules out of one or two experiences (Davis, Eshelman, and McKay 2008, 208–209). Build self-esteem (see chapter 11) and self-love (see chapter 14).

4. *Emotions.* There are two techniques:

    a. Recall the definition of "mindfulness" in the introduction. Release anger and thoughts that spark it by mindfully visualizing each, labeling it (*There's my anger about...*), and releasing it by visualizing it in one of the following ways (McKay, Davis, and Fanning 2011, 130–131; McKay, Wood, and Brantley 2007):

    On leaves floating away on a stream

    On clouds as they breeze by

    On red balloons released into the air

In sand washed away by the waves.

b. Do grief work for the underlying hurt of what you wanted and didn't get.

5. *Physical reactions.* Breathe. Do relaxation exercises. Avoid using alcohol or drugs (illegal or prescription). Get therapeutic assistance if symptoms seem overwhelming.

6. *Desires.* Dwell on your desire to be free of this memory and the anger it sparks. Find gratitude that your ex-partner revealed this untrustworthiness, which allows you to release the relationship. Focus on wanting good relationships in your life.

7. *Actions.* When all else fails, *do* something different. If you still have anger, do volunteer work where you treat others with kindness. Focus on what's good. Behave *as if* you were free of this memory. It will help you grow beyond it in your thoughts and feelings as well. *Remember:*

different actions result in different consequences.

Apply these interventions to your own anger cycle. First, choose an event from the past that you still feel anger around. The visualization Accessing Divorce Anger, Part One (downloadable audio) can help you. Fill out the following: record your present reaction to the past event on the left and your new, defused response on the right.

Event: _____

Old Reaction	change to	Defused Response
Filters:		
Environmental:		
Physical:		
Attitudes and beliefs:		
Interpretations:		
Emotions:		
Surface emotion(s):		
Underlying emotion(s):		
Physical reactions:		
Desires:		
Actions:		

What worked? _____
   Why? _____
What was difficult? _____
   Why? _____
Your reactions: _____

After you work these defusing techniques, there may still be anger about the past that won't go away. Then it's time to take the bomb (carefully!) and blow it up in a safe place away from everyone.

Safe Detonations of Past Anger

The following methods have been effective for many Rebuilding Seminar participants. They have one common denominator: *all are done away from the ex-partner.* It would only raise rage if you were to vent anger about the past at your ex-partner. Keep in mind that you are feeling the anger to let it go, not to ramp it up. After doing this, you'll notice a difference when you see your ex-partner again—less emotional attachment and less likelihood of getting hooked by that person's anger.

1.   Passive techniques:

a. *Destroying copies of old pictures.* Judy taped a picture of her ex-husband to her tire so she could drive to work and see his image tear and crumble.

b. *Fantasizing alternate realities.* Anne dreamed of burning cuss words into her ex-husband's lawn. Burt imagined mowing down his ex-wife's prize flower garden. *Enjoy your fantasies, but don't act them out.*

c. *Letter writing.* Write a series of anger letters. *Do not mail them.* Burn them up or rip them to shreds.

2. Semi-passive techniques:

a. *Screaming.* Scream nasty things into a recorder. Play that back while recording on another recorder. Keep doing this until you've created a whole yelling crowd. Play it back, imagining that it's blasting out of huge speakers at your ex-partner's home at 3:00a.m. Mary found she was angry with herself and would holler into the mirror. When she looked away, she yelled, "Look at me, dammit, when I'm talking to you!" If you must work through anger at yourself, aim it at your behavior. Don't shame yourself.

    b. *Gestalt technique.* Imagine your ex-partner sitting in an empty chair. Give him or her a piece of your mind. Next, sit in that chair and pretend you're the other person answering back, for example, "Well, it was all your fault." Move back and be yourself again. You'll be surprised how much this dialog will release anger, tears, and help you exorcise the relationship from inside you.

3.   Active techniques:

    These release the most anger energy.

    a. *Pounding things.* Clear the furniture away, roll up a bath towel, and beat the rug while screaming your feelings out. Patricia beat the floor furiously. Twenty minutes later she was sweating and angry because she was too tired to beat the towel some more!

    b. *Chop and dig.* Chopping wood can release a tremendous amount of anger energy. Beth dug a mock grave in her garden and buried ashes from burned copies of photos of her ex-partner along with perennial flower bulbs. Her anger became a beautiful flower garden.

   c. *Housework.* Do those dirty chores you've been avoiding. Imagine mopping the floor with your ex or sanding him or her away. You'll make your house cleaner than ever.

   d. *Breaking things.* Susan bought a box of mismatched saucers from the thrift store and broke them on her kitchen floor while cussing. When done, she swept up her anger along with the broken pieces and threw it all away. (Be sure to wear eye protection.)

   e. *Throwing things.* Regina nailed sketches of her ex-husband and his girlfriend to the backyard fence. She threw two dozen eggs at them while screaming. When finished, she washed all the egg "goo" into her garden.

   f. *Physical exercise.* Various ways of working out can be

excellent for releasing anger if you imagine venting at your ex-partner. Be creative. Steve found a globe his ex-partner had given him. He ripped it to shreds with his bare hands. "She destroyed my world," he said. "So, I destroyed hers."

A word about safety: set up anger exercises to do no harm to yourself, any other living thing, or anything of value. Also, be sure you're physically in shape. As with grief, manage your anger by taking specific time to work on it and take breaks. You'll release anger, move toward acceptance of the situation, and feel empowered. Again, do all this work away from your ex-partner.

From these three types of past-anger release, brainstorm what you can do. Try to pick something from each category (passive, semi-passive, active):

1. _____
2. _____
3. _____
4. _____
5. _____
6. _____

These anger techniques are designed for you to let out your anger safely. Give yourself permission. The goal is emotional release that leads toward acceptance and peace about what happened, not further agitation. You'll know you're succeeding when you have fewer thoughts about our ex-partner. Continue to deal with anger using the visualization Accessing Divorce Anger, Part Two (downloadable audio).

Moving Toward the Future

As you let go this anger about the past, you'll find more excitement about the future. Anger energy can help you here as well. Use it to improve your life:
- Go back to school.
- Start a new career.
- Go for that promotion.
- Start a new exercise program (after getting a doctor's review).
- Start a new hobby.
- Save up and take that dream vacation.
- Join a club or organization of a new interest.

Brainstorm productive activities for your anger energy:

1. _____
2. _____
3. _____
4. _____
5. _____
6. _____

Releasing anger about the past is a major step on your healing journey, one that moves you closer to the peace of forgiveness (which is discussed in chapter 10). For now, know this work cannot be skipped; otherwise it tends to come out sideways and sabotage other relationships. The next chapter, "The Power of Anger, Part Two," on becoming assertive, will give steps to releasing current anger.

Journaling to Freedom

Write about your abilities to release your anger about the past. Commit to doing so safely and with purpose.

198

_____
_____
_____
_____
_____
_____
_____
_____

Action Steps for Moving Onward

Share with those close to you about your expression of anger.

1. Complete the exercises in this chapter:

   a. List situations in which you felt angry that had the underlying emotions of frustration, hurt, fear or threat, and inadequacy.

   b. Work through the anger process. Assess your awareness and expression of anger.

   c. Listen to the Accessing Divorce Anger, Part One visualization (downloadable audio) and write

    d. Defuse anger from a past event using the anger cycle.

    e. Do an anger-release brainstorm.

    f. List goals for moving toward the future.

    g. Write a letter to yourself about releasing anger about the past.

    2. Listen to the Accessing Divorce Anger, Part Two visualization (downloadable audio) at least three times this week.

    3. Listen to the Power of Grief and Anger meditation (downloadable audio).

    4. Get with a trusted friend and do one or more of the anger exercises described in this chapter.

    5. Take time away from your anger work to nourish yourself with good food, quiet music, or meditation. You're working hard to heal from your loss.

Part III

Becoming Detached

The next two chapters show you how to release the ended relationship by using anger assertively and letting go with forgiveness to launch you further on your quest to welcome the future instead of dwelling on the pain of the past.

Chapter 9 promotes the healing power of anger to handle current issues around relationship loss and build assertiveness skills for your new life.

Chapter 10 helps you confront loss leftovers and release their hold. Reaching appropriate forgiveness is a gift that frees you from emotional entanglement.

Chapter 9

The Power of Anger, Part Two: Current Anger, Becoming Assertive

That we are is God's gift to us. Who we become is our gift to God.
—Author unknown

STEPS ALONG THE WAY

1. **Styles of Anger Expression**
2. **Removing Blocks to Expressing Anger**
3. **How to Resolve Current Anger**
   - **Defusing Anger**
   - **Becoming Assertive**

There are always circumstances where we have anger, especially during divorce. Recall the main emotions underlying anger: hurt, frustration, fear or threat, and inadequacy. When these emotions arise in current situations, you can feel anger because you aren't getting what you believe you deserve. Knowing how to appropriately resolve current anger is an essential skill to navigate both in divorce and in life.

Many people equate the emotion of anger with the behavior of aggression. But that's only one behavior when angry. Let's look at the behavior styles and determine which one(s) you use.

Styles of Anger Expression

Some externalize anger energy; others internalize it. These can be combined, or you may have different styles in different relationships.
1. *Explosion.* Aggressive words and actions aimed at another person rather than at that person's behavior.
2. *Implosion.* Anger energy turned inward, behaving passively toward others.
    a. *Somatizers.* Anger comes out physically: headaches, high blood pressure, heart or circulatory problems, cancer, gastrointestinal

difficulties, arthritis, among others. There's also depression.

    b. *Self-punishers.* Psychological impairment, especially depression.

3. *Underhanders.* Anger is internalized: first act passive; then later react in sarcastic or sneaky passive-aggressive ways.
4. *Assertive.* Aware of self and others. Respectful expression of anger, focusing on behavior, not at another person.

Note the range of anger style expression as shown on the continuum on the image below.

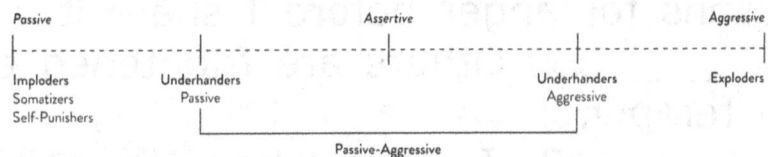

Correlations of Anger Styles to Passive, Assertive, Aggressive Behavior

To determine your style(s), put a checkmark next to the statements that are true or mostly true for you:

_____ 1. When angry, I've hit someone or broken something.

_____ 2. I feel depressed and don't know why.

_____ 3. When stressed, I get headaches.

_____ 4. I withdraw when I don't get my way.

_____ 5. I speak with others about my anger.

_____ 6. I call other people names when I'm angry.

_____ 7. I feel guilty when I'm angry.

_____ 8. My muscles tighten up for no apparent reason.

_____ 9. I use humor to get back at others.

_____ 10. I think through my reasons for anger before I share it.

_____ 11. Others are frightened by my temper.

_____ 12. I smile when I'm angry and pretend I don't feel that way.

_____ 13. I find it hard to relax.

_____ 14. I'll be late when I'm angry.

_____ 15. I wait for the appropriate time to share my feelings.

_____ 16. I stuff my feelings and then blow off steam to release them.

_____ 17. When someone is angry at me, I don't know what to do.

_____ 18. My stomach churns when I'm emotional.

_____ 19. I feel angry when those close to me don't guess my desires.

_____ 20. I listen to others even when they're angry with me.

_____ 21. I've damaged job prospects and friendships with my anger.

_____ 22. It's hard for me to forgive myself for mistakes.

_____ 23. I can joke my way out of anything.

_____ 24. I work with others to resolve disagreements.

Key: Exploder: 1, 6, 11, 16, 21; Somatizer: 3, 8, 13, 18; Self-punisher: 2, 7, 12, 17, 22; Underhander: 4, 9, 14, 19, 23; Assertive: 5, 10, 15, 20, 24.

Your two top styles:

1. _____
2. _____

Your reactions: _____

Recognition and ownership are the beginnings of change. *Do not* blame others for your reactions. You may feel anger for any number of reasons, but what you do with it is your conscious choice.

Will's Take Before my divorce, I had great difficulty being aware of anger. My wife said she could tell I was angry, and it would take me two days to get in touch with it. She was right. Two days later I was furious! I needed to work on finding my anger. From then on, when I didn't like something, I'd search my feelings for anger. After a while, I got to a one-day delay. Finally, I could feel my anger while the situation was happening.

Removing the Blocks to Anger Expression

Some people are "anger avoiders" (Potter-Efron and Potter-Efron 2006). They either block out their awareness of anger or hold back its expression. The following are anger blocks (Fisher and Alberti 2016) and what you need to break through the block toward healthy anger expression. These anger blocks apply to both anger about the

past and current anger. Rate yourself, 1–10.
1. Fear
   a. *Fear of losing control:* _____
   Accept you're angry. Stifling anger can fuel violence or illness. Release anger without endangering yourself or others.
   b. *Fear of retaliation:* _____
   This is realistic for those ending an abusive relationship. For most, it's the covert threat of withdrawal, legal entanglements, or custody fights that prompts fear of anger. Use anger energy to validate and protect yourself. This fosters self-respect.
   c. *Fear of rejection:* _____
   This is a disentanglement issue. Becoming angry may remove leftover denial. Dwell in reality. Anger can help you do that.
2. *Appearances:* _____
"Anger is bad," and "you're only as big as those things that make you angry," promote attempts to be above it all when you're really seething. This doesn't help.

3. *Traumatic family experiences:* _____

An emotionally or physically abusive family teaches acting out anger destructively or shutting anger inside. Neither is productive. Choose awareness and appropriate expression. Those abused as children can use anger to release the shame of being victimized.

4. *Lack of awareness:* _____

Many people are emotionally out of touch or don't know what to do with anger and don't understand it's a normal response. Learn to express it appropriately.

Which are your highest blocks? _____

_____

Your reactions: _____

_____

How to Resolve Current Anger

Much of what we explored in chapter 8 about releasing anger about the past applies here: how anger is generated; anger awareness; filters, thoughts,

feelings, and needs that make up the anger cycle; and the steps of the anger process:
1. Recognize that you are angry.
2. Identify the source.
3. Understand the basic reasons.
4. Deal with anger realistically.

This last point is the difference between anger about the past and current anger. With current anger, you must handle both the emotion and the situation at hand. It does no good to release anger energy by yourself and then return to the same problem at home, work, or with a neighbor. Venting anger at someone will likely escalate the situation. What can you do? Two steps:
1. Defuse your anger energy so you can make decisions about the situation:
   a. Perhaps you'll let go of your anger by changing expectations and attitudes.
   b. Perhaps you'll realize you must communicate your anger and ask another to change behavior.
2. If interaction is needed, assertiveness is an excellent tool

to help you. The last section will focus on both of these steps.

Defusing Current Anger

Research indicates that venting current anger can increase rather than decrease its energy (Alberti and Emmons 2017). Here's a better approach:

1. Come to an acceptance of your anger. Rather than let it fuel reaction, allow it to teach you its lessons: your attachments, the needs for protection and change, underlying emotions, and the desire to come into harmony.
2. Understand and actively intervene in your anger cycle in much the same way you did for anger about the past in chapter 8. Let's look at an anger cycle for a current anger and see how it can be defused.

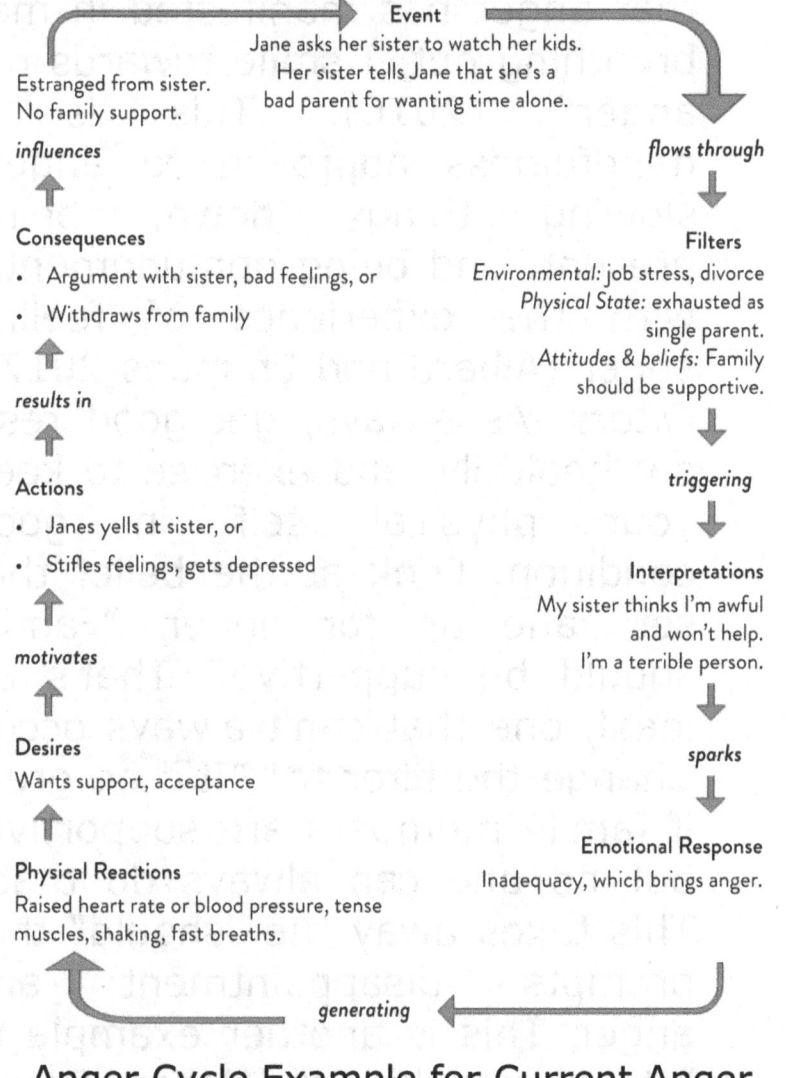

Anger Cycle Example for Current Anger

1. *Event.* Standing away from the event, Jane can use the mindfulness techniques to relax and get grounded. As Vietnamese Zen master Thich Nhat Hanh suggests, "Breathing in, I know

that anger has manifested in me; breathing out, I smile towards my anger" (2016). This is a mindfulness approach to anger: slowing things down, being present, and being nonjudgmental with the experience of feeling anger (Alberti and Emmons 2017).

2. *Filters.* As always, get good rest, eat healthily, and exercise to keep your physical self in good condition. Look at the belief that set Jane up for anger, "Family should be supportive." That's an ideal, one that can't always occur. Change the filter to: "It'd be great if family members are supportive, but no one can always do that." This takes away the "should" that prompts disappointment and anger. This is another example of "stress inoculation" (McKay, Davis, and Fanning 2011).

3. *Interpretations.* Jane's assumption that her sister thinks she's awful only dumps on herself. Coping thoughts can move Jane away from self-recrimination, for example, "Assuming my sister's

motives or attaching my self-image to her opinions only causes problems. Maybe she's stressed and watching my kids adds to it. I don't know her real reasons. If she doesn't tell me, that's her problem not mine." This helps Jane avoid the anger distortion of mind-reading (Davis, Eshelman, and McKay 2008).

4. *Emotions.* There are two techniques:

    a. Jane can send her anger away with mindfulness techniques ("There's my anger about...") and release the thoughts as floating leaves, clouds blowing by, a released balloon, or similar (McKay, Davis, and Fanning 2011; McKay, Wood, and Brantley 2007).

    b. Jane can confront the deeper emotion of inadequacy and focus on other ways to get support.

5. *Physical reactions.* Jane can breathe. Do relaxation exercises, avoid using alcohol or drugs (illegal or prescription) to relax. She can marshal her resources to

devise plans and carry them out to meet her needs.

For desires and actions, Jane can learn to act assertively.

Nina Remembers... *During a Rebuilding weekend, at the end of our session on anger, a soft-spoken, wise Asian woman shared her favorite Chinese proverb: "If you are patient in one moment of anger, you will escape a hundred days of sorrow."*

Acting Assertively

The late Dr. Wayne Dyer (2001) wrote, "We teach others how to treat us." *If you don't like how someone treats you, you must teach him or her to treat you differently.* Assertiveness is the essential skill to help you. It will guide you to respect others as well. First, let's define unhealthy and healthy behaviors and then apply assertiveness to realistic resolution of current anger.

Behavior Definitions and Contrasts
1. *Passive:*
    a. "I'm not okay; you're okay."
    b. Low self-worth or denial.
    c. Unmet desires lead to beliefs of victimhood.

d. Actions that sabotage self: avoiding conflict, allowing others to violate boundaries.

e. Relationship types: nurturing parent giving to others and not self, irresponsible natural child.

2. *Aggressive:*

a. "I'm okay; you're not okay," while questioning, "Am I okay?" Attacks before others find out about inner "deficiencies."

b. Low self-worth or defensiveness.

c. Desires become demands: believes in "win-lose" and wants to "win," becoming a persecutor.

d. Actions that damage others.

e. Relationship types: condemning critical parent, manipulating adaptive child.

3. *Passive-aggressive:*

a. "I'm not okay; you're not okay." Thinks others are more important until they act out through covert or overt aggression.

b. Low self-worth, futility, frustration.

c. Invisible desires become demands: after getting trampled, demand their needs be met. As "victim," see persecuting others as only way out.

    d. Actions that sabotage self, damage others.

    e. Relationship type: covertly controlling nurturing parent (martyr), manipulating adaptive child.

4. *Assertive:*

    a. "I'm okay, and you're okay," a positive self-image, high personal power.

    b. High self-worth.

    c. Negotiates desires to meet needs while taking others' needs into account: "win-win."

    d. Actions build healthy relationships: own thoughts, feelings, and desires; cooperative.

    e. Relationship type: adult.

The goal is to be assertive in all relationships. Ask yourself: "How do others treat me? How do I treat others?" For the following, make a checkmark under each column for their behavior toward you and your behavior toward them. Use this assessment in two ways: (1) Realize where you are less assertive to find patterns and make changes. (2) See where you are assertive; maintain that behavior and use it in other relationships.

Relationship Category	Passive		Passive-Aggressive		Aggressive		Assertive	
	Toward You	Your Behavior	Toward You	Your Behavior	Toward You	Your Behavior	Toward You	Your Behavior
1. Father								
2. Mother								
3. Love partner								
4. Opposite sex								
5. Boss								
6. Subordinates								
7. Siblings								
8. My children								
9. Those you want to impress								
10. Friends								
11. People older than you								
12. Those younger than you								
13. Strangers								
14.								
15.								

What patterns emerge? _____

_____

What relationships do you want to change and why (to be treated differently, treat others differently)?
_____
_____
_____
_____

Effects of Becoming Assertive
When you change from passive or aggressive behavior to assertive, you and others in your life will be affected:
1. *What you do influences the outcome* even if you don't get what you desire.
2. *You must cope with others' desires to keep you the same.* Because many people approach change with discomfort, teaching others to change their behavior toward you won't be easy. They'll try to keep you the same so their world will stay predictable.
   • Passive people who become assertive often get feedback that they're aggressive.

- Aggressive individuals who become more assertive may find others see them as passive.
- Those who are already assertive will celebrate your healthy changes.

No matter how assertive you are, there's no guarantee you'll accomplish what you seek. Even so, you'll always get these rewards:
- Increased self-worth.
- Better management of anger and other emotions.
- Stronger personal power.
- Reinforced adult ego state.
- More likely to establish healthier relationships since assertive communication is essential to them.

Assertiveness Components

Based on the excellent book *Your Perfect Right: Assertiveness and Equality in Your Life and Relationships* by Robert E. Alberti, PhD, and Michael L. Emmons, PhD, (2017) and other sources, the following is a basic list of assertiveness components, both verbal and nonverbal.

Nonverbal components. It's generally accepted that how the message is presented in more important rather than the actual words used (Alberti and Emmons 2017). On a scale of 1 (low) to 10 (high), rate your current overall effectiveness of these nonverbal components.

1. Distance: appropriate space between you and other person	
2. Body posture: stand, sit up straight	
3. Physical contact: operate within your and others' comfort zones	
4. Eye contact: neither staring nor unable to engage	
5. Facial expression: matches your emotion and message	
6. Voice tone, inflection, volume: matches your emotion and message	
7. Fluency: even, understandable, neither too fast or slow	
8. Gestures: add to your message rather than detract	
9. Timing: communicate when that respects both your message and the other person	
10. Listening: give feedback, confirm your understanding of other's message	

What are the top three nonverbal components you need to improve?

1. _____
2. _____
3. _____

How have these affected your communication? _____

Verbal components. These have to do with content. Two factors are most important:
1. *Remain issue focused.* Remember, relationships are the behaviors between individuals. The assertive person stays focused on the partner's behavior.
2. *Own your thoughts, feelings, desires, and actions.* Use "I-messages" as mentioned by Dr. Thomas Gordon (2008). These emphasize the speaker's ownership of thoughts and feelings about the topic instead of blaming the other person. For example: "I think your idea needs work," instead of "You are wrong," or "I get afraid when I see you do that," instead of "You scare me." Without I-messages, the issue tends to go unresolved, and personal attacks can result. How you talk reflects how you think and see yourself in the world. I-messages will remind you that it's *your* anger, *your* grief, or *your* happiness, and that *you* are responsible for dealing with them.

On a scale of 1 (low) to 10 (high), rate your current overall effectiveness for each verbal assertiveness component.

1. Remain issue-focused: discuss behavior, not person	
2. Own your thoughts, feelings, desires, and actions	
3. Use I-messages	

What do you need to work on most?
_____

Communication is about shared meaning. Assertiveness is the best pathway to achieve it. The assertive person considers the needs of both talker and listener and strives not to end a conversation unless there's mutual understanding.

Assertiveness Attitudes
1. *Be assertive with yourself.*
    a. Consider what must be discussed.
    b. Determine your thoughts, feelings, desires, and willingness to act.
    c. Decide whom to approach.
    d. Plan how to respectfully approach that person and topic.

Remember, in each interaction, you teach others how you want to be treated.

2. *Assertiveness encompasses the full range of behavior, from extreme action to doing nothing.* A choice to remain inactive to determine the best course of action is being assertive. In extreme situations, you may need to act aggressively, for example someone steps on your toe and doesn't hear your request to move. A slight push may be appropriate to alleviate the pain.

3. *Sometimes, you must let go of what others may think.* Healthy assertiveness is a blend of self-consideration and respect for others. If asking for your needs to be met is contrary to another's desires, your communication can be respectful. Don't sell yourself short; let your values guide you.

4. *Avoid "hard" assertiveness* in which you only consider your needs and not those of others.

On a scale of 1 (low) to 10 (high), rate your current overall effectiveness for each:

1. Assertive with yourself	
a. Focus on topic	
b. Understand your position (thoughts, feelings, desires, actions)	
c. Consider whom to approach	
d. Consider best way to approach	
2. Flexible behavior, can take actions or remain inactive	
3. Not ruled by others' opinions:	
a. Can take other people's thoughts and feelings into account	
b. Assertively set boundaries and make requests	

What are three areas you need to develop?

1. _____
2. _____
3. _____

Putting Assertiveness into Action

The following frameworks based on Cooley and Hollandsworth (1977; Alberti and Emmons 2017, 93) are simple and effective ways to structure assertive interactions. Be assertive with yourself first. Use I-messages and be mindful of the nonverbal and verbal components.

Asking for Change, Assistance, or Asserting Rights

1. *State the problem.* Rate it on a scale of 1 (low importance) to 10 (high importance).
2. *Make your request.* Share your thoughts and feelings about the topic. Express what you want or don't want, and what you need.
3. *Listen to the other person's response.*
4. *Get clear understanding.* Repeat the other person's position and what has been agreed to. Ask the other person to do the same.

Let's look at how Jane can assertively approach her sister. Jane's sister, Beth, dismisses Jane's need for assistance with her kids and said Jane was a bad parent for needing alone time. Jane takes time to think through the best way to talk with her sister. She still needs help with her kids, but she also wants to connect positively with Beth. Here's how she uses the framework.

1. *State the problem and rating.* "Beth, I'm confused about our discussion on me needing alone

time. I'd like to talk with you about it. On a scale of 1 to 10, this is a 9, so it's very important to me."

2. *Request.* "Yesterday, I asked if you could watch my kids for an afternoon. You said no and commented that I was a bad parent for needing alone time. It's not like you to respond this way. I understand if you can't help. But I felt angry when you said this to me. I don't want us to be distanced from each other. I really want to know if anything's going on in your life that's stressful that might have influenced our talk. I'd like us to support each other."

3. *Listen.* Jane listens to Beth. (Beth shares the stress she's been having as a parent and apologizes for her statement to Jane.) Jane asks questions to understand her.

4. *Get clear understanding.* "Okay, now I understand what's been going on with you. I know your kids and mine can be a handful. How about I watch yours for a time, and then you can watch

mine? Or, we could get a joint babysitter so we can both get some time away. What do you think?"

Beth may or may not be responsive. Regardless, *Jane has been appropriately assertive and can feel good about her effort* (which is all she's responsible for anyway). A clear agreement can be the basis of more discussion if difficulties arise. More importantly, after Beth's cooperation, Jane can express appreciation and reinforce future support. (For the most complete assertiveness skill, I highly recommend *Core Communication: Maps, Skills and Processes* by Sherod and Phyllis Miller, see http://www.couplecommunication.com.)

Choose an issue where you need to discuss a change in behavior or make a request. Then, plan the steps:

1. State the problem and rating: _____

2. Request: _____

3. Listen (State how you will listen.):
_____
_____

4. Get clear understanding (State how you will ask.): _____
_____

Apply this framework to three different situations. This will help you to be assertive with yourself first. Use the visualization Asking for Change, Assistance, or Asserting Rights, available at http://www.newharbinger.com/45397. Return to it when you need to be assertive, especially for current anger situations.

Maintaining Assertive Decisions or Saying "No"

1. *Listen to the other person's position* and teach him or her, through your attentiveness, to listen to you. Ask questions until you are sure you understand.
2. *Determine your position.* Ask for time to think, letting others know you respect them, their message, and yourself.

3. *State your position.* Use I-messages. This may be a simple "no" or a more complete explanation. Giving your reason should never water down your position.
4. *Express understanding* by empathizing with others' requests even if you decline. Connect with them as human beings. This may include brainstorming solutions, but don't be manipulated into changing your basic position.

Example: Bob only hears from Cheryl when she wants his help. Whenever he'd like to see her, she's unavailable. He feels used. Now, Cheryl phones to ask him if she can use his car to go to see a friend while her car is being repaired.

1. *Listen.* Bob listens attentively to Cheryl's request to borrow his car. He asks any questions he needs to fully understand her.
2. *Determine position.* Bob says that he needs to think this over. He considers that his car is almost new. Mindful that he needs to

back away from Cheryl, Bob decides to say no.
3. *State position.* Bob calls Cheryl and says, "I know you'd like to see your friend while your car is serviced. However, my car is still pretty new, and I don't feel comfortable loaning it to anyone."
4. *Express understanding.* "I know that you've had this plan to see your friend for over a month and just yesterday your car broke down. But, my car won't be available."

Cheryl may still try to get Bob's car. Maintaining his position helps Bob respect his needs while treating Cheryl respectfully. This is also a positive step in his disentanglement from their friendship.

Consider a decision you've made that another person is trying to change, or think of a request made of you or is likely to be made. Plan the steps of what to do and say.
1. *Listen* (State what you prepare to do.): _____

2. *Determine position* (As best you can, what is your position now? Be open to change as you listen to other person.): _____

_____

3. *State position* (How might you share your point of view?):_____

_____

4. *Express understanding* (State what you prepare to do.): _____

   Choose three completely different situations and apply this framework. Keep it handy for future issues. Use the Maintaining Assertive Decisions or Saying No visualization (the downloadable audio is available at http://www.newharbinger.com/45397) to assist your assertiveness. Return to it as often as you need to program success in your relationships with others.

Journaling to Freedom

Write a letter to the world about your courage and strength to be a healthy, assertive person who's willing to treat others and self with respect.

_____
_____
_____
_____
_____
_____
_____

Becoming assertive helps you detach from your ended love relationship and grow into your new life. The next chapter will explore the process of letting go, using forgiveness as a profound step in healing.

Action Steps for Moving Onward
1. Determine your style of expressing anger.
2. Assess your blocks to anger awareness and expression.

3. Assess your assertiveness in the relationships in your life. Share the results with a trusted friend and get feedback.

4. Assess your use of nonverbal and verbal components of assertiveness.

5. Use the frameworks discussed in Asking for Change, Assistance, or Asserting Rights and Maintaining Assertive Decisions or Saying No to analyze a recent situation and what you might have done differently. Plan how to be assertive in three present or possible future interactions. Role-play with a trusted friend any situation where you need further assistance using the assertiveness components.

6. Contemplate both assertiveness visualizations (downloadable audio files) at any time you need to prepare for a situation in which you want to be assertive.

7. Listen to the What Can I Do? meditation (downloadable audio).

8. Write your letter about being assertive and share with a trusted friend.

9. Do something satisfying to celebrate your hard work in self-improvement. Make it fun!

Chapter 10

Letting Go to Reach Forgiveness

When patterns are broken, new worlds emerge.
—Tuli Kupferberg

STEPS ALONG THE WAY

1. **Where Are You Stuck?**
2. **How Are You Stuck?**
3. **The Art of Disentanglement**
4. **Appropriate Forgiveness**

Many people believe the physical end of the relationship completes letting go. That's not true. Without emotional detachment, one can remain stuck in grief, anger, and loneliness, and new relationships will be endangered by these leftovers. Two major goals of divorce recovery are disentanglement and forgiveness. This chapter will help you reach them.

Where Are You Stuck?

Rate your divorce-recovery progress for the issues of abandonment, woundedness, and detachment according to the following scale:

```
0    1    2    3    4    5    6    7    8    9    10
```
I feel stuck and can't seem to get going.   I feel better and cope some of the time.   I feel great and am moving on with my life.

Abandonment Issues	
1. Denial	
2. Fear	
3. Loneliness	
Woundedness Issues	
1. Grief	
2. Damaged	
Unlovable	
Rejection	
Guilt	
3. Past anger	
Detachment Issues	
1. Current anger	
2. Disentanglement	

Which three have the lowest scores? _____
_____

Which three have the highest scores? _____
_____

Your reaction: _____
_____

While it's tempting to dwell on how far you have to go, always acknowledge and celebrate your growth. Return to this and mark your progress.

How Are You Stuck?

The feeling of being stuck can occur in thoughts, feelings, desires, and behaviors. Examples:

Issue: Grief

Repeated thoughts: *I'll never stop crying. No one will love me like my ex-partner.*

Stuck feelings: Devastation, despair, depression.

Unrealistic desires: Don't want to cry. Want ex-partner to return. Wish hurt would go away.

Negatively reinforcing behavior: Avoid grief through excessive alcohol or drug use, work constantly or become a busyholic, or have short-term unsatisfying affairs. Alternatively, crying constantly and avoiding others.

Issue: Anger

Repeated thoughts: *How dare my partner leave! I want to get back at her or him. Can't handle anger.*

Stuck feelings: Rage, depression.

Unrealistic desires: Want to make life miserable for ex. Want to take ex for everything he's or she's got.

Negatively reinforcing behavior: Call ex-partner at all hours. Sneak into old house and remove items. Fight in court over everything. Alienate others.

Assess the ways you remain entangled. Choose three issues you gave the lowest rating in your divorce-recovery progress. Do more if you feel the need.

Issue: _____ **Rating:** _____

Repeated thoughts: _____

Stuck feelings: _____
Unrealistic desires: _____

Negatively reinforcing behavior: _____

Issue: _____ **Rating:** _____
Repeated thoughts: _____

Stuck feelings: _____
Unrealistic desires: _____

Negatively reinforcing behavior: _____

Issue: _____ **Rating:** _____
Repeated thoughts: _____

Stuck feelings: _____
Unrealistic desires: _____

Negatively reinforcing behavior: _____

Your reactions: _____

Now, let's learn how to let these go.

The Art of Disentanglement

Disentanglement is "a state of being whereby the complications of involvement are removed." Wouldn't you like this to be true for you? To remove the complications as well as the involvement itself, know where you're headed. Listen to the When Your Disentanglement Is Complete visualization, available at http://www.newharbinger.com/45397. If this visualization proves to be difficult, come back to it after you've done the exercises in this chapter.

These three steps will help you disentangle.

1. Understand the positive and negative behaviors of the relationship.
2. Alter your inner experience of the ended relationship.
3. Set boundaries in your emotions, behavior, and interactions.

These lead to complete disentanglement through appropriate forgiveness.

The Positives and Negatives of Your Ended Relationship

Be completely honest about your love relationship. Make lists using simple phrases to describe behavior and patterns in it. These will set a boundary around what occurred, separating it from your new life beyond divorce. (List the top five. Do more as you desire.)

The "Good"
1. Your healthy, loving behaviors, for example, "I was a good listener."

1. _____
2. _____
3. _____
4. _____
5. _____

2. Ex-partner's healthy, loving behaviors, for example, "My partner helped with household chores."

   1. _____
   2. _____
   3. _____
   4. _____
   5. _____

3. How you grew as a person, for example, "I learned to stand up for myself."

   1. _____
   2. _____
   3. _____
   4. _____
   5. _____

The "Bad"

1. Your actions that were unhealthy, neglectful, or abusive to your former partner, for example, "I was often late when we met somewhere."

   1. _____
   2. _____
   3. _____
   4. _____
   5. _____

2. Your former love partner's actions that were unhealthy, neglectful, or abusive to you, for example, "My partner bought expensive items without consulting me."

   1. _____
   2. _____
   3. _____
   4. _____
   5. _____

The "Ugly"

These are unhealthy patterns you both engaged in, for example, "We didn't discuss problems until one of us blew up."

   1. _____
   2. _____
   3. _____
   4. _____
   5. _____

These lists give perspective:
1. Acknowledging the positive fosters kindness toward yourself and toward your ex-partner. This counteracts bitterness. Also, awareness of healthy aspects encourages you to seek them in a future relationship.

2. You take responsibility for your actions. This helps you avoid re-creating the same problems with someone else.
3. Recognizing unhealthy behaviors and destructive patterns helps you avoid the emotional entanglement of perseverating on what you enjoyed in the relationship.
4. These lists also help you set appropriate boundaries within yourself and with your ex-partner.

Alter Your Inner Experience

Disentanglement is *a balance between not avoiding* the issues, objects, or individuals who spark your pain *and not wallowing* in that pain or pursuing those relationships. How? Change your thoughts and emotions about the relationship. This keeps you from becoming stuck in between yearning or avoiding.

Changing Thoughts and Feelings

You're going to apply mindfulness to those repeated thoughts and feelings that keep you emotionally entangled with your ex-partner. Take a deep breath, close your eyes, and let those thoughts and feelings resurface. Don't judge them or try to hold them back. Simply be with them...

Catalog the first six that came to mind.

Thoughts:

1. _____
2. _____
3. _____
4. _____
5. _____
6. _____

Feelings:

1. _____
2. _____
3. _____
4. _____
5. _____
6. _____

I'll bet you noticed that thoughts brought up feelings, and feelings brought up more thoughts. That's okay. These are linked for everyone. Let's examine how this thought-feeling linkage works. The following are simple summaries, yet they lead to useful detaching practices. Choose any one or more of the thoughts or feelings you listed before and try these three approaches to help you disentangle. Work them until you feel relief.

Mindfulness

Mindfulness helps you connect better with yourself and meet your physical and emotional needs. It also helps you avoid staying stuck in painful emotions. (Narang 2014). To release troublesome thoughts and feelings, mindfully visualize each, label it, and release it as you did in chapter 8 on anger (McKay, Davis, and Fanning 2011, 130–131): There's my thought (or feeling) of _____:
- Floating away on a leaf in a stream
- Going past the window of my car on a billboard
- Released on a red balloon into the air
- Rattling by on the side of a boxcar at a railroad crossing

Rational Emotive Behavior Therapy: Reframing

Recall from chapter 8 how we process experience (Ellis 1975):

Event → Interpretation → Emotion

Our emotions are not based on the event itself but on the interpretation (meaning) we give to the event.

Example:

Event: Divorce

Interpretations: Divorce has ruined me. I'll never survive.

Feelings: Fear, grief, anger, depression, hopelessness.

To demonstrate how interpretations, not the event, spark our emotions, consider this change:

Event: Divorce

Interpretations: Divorce is difficult, but I'm going to make it. I'm learning to live better.

Feelings: Some grief and anger, but also determination, hope, and optimism.

This "reframing" shift is at the core of the entire rebuilding blocks divorce-recovery program. Change your thoughts to alter your emotions. Example: Consider the person who blames self for having been abused emotionally or physically in the relationship. Reframing might look like this:

Old Viewpoint

Thoughts: *I caused my partner to hurt me because I couldn't do anything right.*

Feelings: Shame, guilt, hurt, humiliation.

New Viewpoint

Thoughts: *I didn't deserve to be abused. This was caused by the other person, not me. I won't ever let this happen again.*

Feelings: Anger, protectiveness, determination.

You can even use reframing to choose alternative ways of defining your ex-partner's behavior.

Old Viewpoint

Thoughts: *My ex-partner was a mean, angry person.*

Feelings: Fear, anger, vengeful.

A Second Viewpoint

Thoughts: *My ex-partner was abused by others and learned to be an abuser.*

Feelings: Anger, understanding.

A Third Viewpoint

Thoughts: *My partner is mentally ill.*

Feelings: Anger, compassion, sadness.

While you should set a firm boundary to avoid such a person, possibly all three interpretations and accompanying emotions have validity.

Changing interpretations and thereby your emotions can help you remove either-or viewpoints that keep you entangled. This process will also hasten closure and bring you toward peace.

Examine the bad and ugly lists and reframe three items. (Do more as you can.)
1. Name a problematic event.
2. Describe your original viewpoint:
    a. Thoughts about yourself, your partner, or actions at the time.
    b. Feelings that arose during that time.
3. Create two alternative viewpoints (more if you like). For each, describe:
    a. Alternative thoughts about yourself, partner, or actions.
    b. Feelings that arise from these new thoughts.

Notice how your feelings change and that this tends to deepen your understanding of the experience.
1. Event: _____

a. *Original viewpoint*
Thoughts: _____

Feelings: _____

b. *Alternative viewpoint #1*
Thoughts: _____

Feelings: _____

c. *Alternative viewpoint #2*
Thoughts: _____

Feelings: _____

2. Event: _____

a. *Original viewpoint*
Thoughts: _____

Feelings: _____

b. *Alternative viewpoint #1*
Thoughts: _____

Feelings: _____

c. *Alternative viewpoint #2*
Thoughts: _____

Feelings: _____

3. Event

a. *Original viewpoint*
Thoughts: _____

Feelings: _____

b. *Alternative viewpoint #1*
Thoughts: _____

Feelings: _____

c. *Alternative viewpoint #2*
   Thoughts: _____

   Feelings: _____

   Your reactions to these exercises:

Emotional Schema Therapy

The emotional schema therapy of Robert Leahy (Leahy, Tirch, and Napolitano 2011) takes reframing even further:

> Event → Interpretation → Emotion → Thoughts (about emotion) → Emotion (sparked by those thoughts about emotion)

Leahy asserts that individuals have "schemas," ways of conceptualizing and strategizing, that frame their interpretation and emotional responses to the world. Here's an example:

   Event: A friend who said he'd drop by doesn't show up.
   Interpretation: I'm going to be alone today.
   Feeling: Loneliness.
   Thoughts about feeling: *I don't like feeling lonely. What's wrong*

with me? I'll probably be lonely for the rest of my life.

Feelings from thoughts about feeling: Despair, hopelessness.

To make a positive change here, you could change your interpretations of the event (reframing), or you could alter how you interpret your feelings (schema):

Event: A friend who said he'd drop by doesn't show up.

Interpretation: I'm going to be alone today.

Feeling: Loneliness.

Thoughts about the feeling: *I don't like feeling lonely, but that's normal because I was looking forward to seeing my friend. Oh well, I'll contact someone else or just go out and about.*

Feelings that follow these last thoughts: Acceptance of lonely feelings. Determination and excitement to do something else.

Leahy (2020, 58–65) makes it clear that changing your schema and your approach to thoughts and feelings will change your experience. He encourages

us to live realistically. Among his "wise strategies" are:
- Everyone experiences difficult and unpleasant emotions.
- Our beliefs (thoughts) about emotions can either make things difficult or help us tolerate them.
- Being realistic about emotions means you won't feel happy all the time. Disappointments are inevitable.
- Be flexible about what is satisfying.

Alter your approach to emotions. Do this by choosing three feelings from the divorce-recovery list you made before. For each, give your interpretation of that feeling. Then, give an accepting interpretation of that feeling as part of being alive. Example:

>Feeling: Fear that I'll never be loved again.
>
>Old interpretation of feeling: I'm unlovable, and no one will ever want me.
>
>New interpretation of feeling: Fear after divorce is normal. I've been afraid before, and it didn't last, nor did it damage my whole life. I can feel fear, but that doesn't

mean it will last forever or that I'll always be unlovable. Only one person left my life, not everyone.

Feeling: _____
Old interpretation of feeling: _____

New interpretation of feeling: _____

Feeling: _____
Old interpretation of feeling: _____

New interpretation of feeling: _____

Feeling: _____
Old interpretation of feeling: _____

New interpretation of feeling: _____

What changes did you notice? _____

How did these affect your emotions of entanglement? _____

Your reactions: _____

(For a very accessible guide to emotional schema therapy, read *Don't Believe Everything You Feel: A CBT Workbook to Identify Your Emotional Schemas and Find Freedom from Anxiety and Depression* by Robert Leahy.)

Set Boundaries
Boundaries in Emotions
1.   *Grief* ("*sad time*")
As discussed in chapter 7, gather items that bring up grief. Take a special time to grieve. Set a timer for twenty minutes. Take breaks to help you manage the emotion.
2.   *Anger* ("*mad time*")
Do the same for anger, as discussed in chapter 8: set aside objects that spark anger. Use the good, bad, and ugly lists, especially the other person's hurtful behavior and unhealthy patterns. Manage your anger by taking regular breaks to refresh yourself. Don't overdo physical activity.
What items can you use for your sad and mad times?

Sad time: _____
_____
_____

Mad time: _____
_____
_____

Will's Take *Remember the one class member who looked at the videos from the last ten Christmases to work through his grief? It was tough, but he felt deeply relieved afterward. For heavy grieving like this, it really helps to have a friend with you.*

3. *Feelings of love and attachment*

Make a list of the ways in which you may still feel emotional attachment to your ex-partner. Use it in your sad time or mad time work. Dumping it on paper helps you cease dwelling on it.

_____   _____
_____   _____
_____   _____
_____   _____

4. *Reinforce positive feelings ("glad time")*

Consider the positive changes and opportunities divorce brings. Reflect on happiness and excitement about your new life. At first, you may only be able to do this a little. As you heal, you'll increase this time as sad time and mad time decrease.

Encourage glad time to filter into your life. Display new mementos and photographs of you and new friends in prominent view. Put energy into physical fitness, new hobbies, and arranging your living environment. Celebrate!

Right now, what do you feel glad about? (It could be: "I'm glad I don't have to put with _____ from my ex anymore.") Add to this list as you disentangle.

_____
_____
_____
_____

Boundaries in Behavior
1.   *Releasing memories*
Create new memories to release the connections that places, friendships, and

holidays have with your ended relationship.
- Go with a friend to that favorite restaurant. Hike with new friends along your "special" trail.
- Create new rituals. Mary suspended the Christmas tree upside down from the ceiling. (Her children loved it!)
- Reestablish friendships. Don't assume a particular friend will close you out. If you still have commonalities, take the risk to build a better friendship.

Where and with whom can I create new memories? _____

What new rituals can I create? _____

What friends can I reconnect with? _____

2. *Manage nurturing behavior*

Some individuals continue nurturing their ex-partner, for example, fixing the car, listening to problems. Others nurture out of guilt. Either way, it keeps you entangled. Instead, nurture yourself: take classes, plant a garden, advance your career, volunteer.

If you find yourself wanting to please your ex-partner, make a list of how that person is not meeting your needs now. This can cause more anger to surface. Use it appropriately to pull away.

_____
_____
_____
_____

Setting Boundaries in Interactions with Ex-Partner: Managing Meetings
1. Keep a journal of topics and questions. Determine what's essential. Only dialog about those at prescribed times unless there's truly an emergency.
2. Agree ahead of time to an agenda of one to three items. Keep it simple.
3. Stick to your agenda. End the conversation or meeting if the

other person won't cooperate. Teach him or her that your discussions must be rational or not at all. (See chapter 9 on assertiveness.)

With a trusted friend at your side, work through the Cutting Heartstrings visualization at http://www.newharbinger.com/45397.

Will's Take *Disentanglement can surprise you. Mark shared, "I haven't thought about her for three days, and I used to think about her all day every day." Julie realized, "This past weekend was the first good one I've had in six months. I'm feeling freer all the time." Letting go allows you to experience life beyond divorce. As Aaron said, "I got up yesterday morning and felt so damn depressed. Then, I realized my depression had nothing to do with my divorce, and I felt great!"*

While disentanglement brings you a measure of peace, more complete relief is grounded in forgiveness when you can say: "I let go of this relationship, understanding what was my part and what was my ex-partner's part. I forgive us both for what we said and did, and for what we didn't say and didn't do." Appropriate forgiveness is profound reframing, which allows you to fully release connection to your ex-partner.

Appropriate Forgiveness

1. *Perceive the reality of loss and acknowledge feelings of betrayal.* Begin by recognizing your relationship is over and life has changed. Acknowledge feelings: betrayal, fear, loneliness, grief, and anger. You've already done much work on these.
2. *Acknowledge, but do not act out, feelings of revenge.* When hurt, it's human nature to feel vengeful. However, acting it out is only destructive.
3. *Heal the feelings.* Each time you work through your emotions of loss, you move closer to appropriate forgiveness.
4. *Reach appropriate forgiveness.* This forgiveness does *not* mean:
    • That what happened in the relationship was okay. If it was

hurtful then, it wouldn't be acceptable now.

- That you are going to forget what happened. Many important lessons were learned at great cost.

However, you can let go of the painful experience while remaining aware of new knowledge.

Ultimately, appropriate forgiveness is a gift for yourself. It frees you to love again. It also opens your heart to unity with life and a sense of at-one-ment (atonement) that relieves fear, pain, and loss. Forgiveness is the most powerful affirmation of a loving being; experience it by listening to the Appropriate Forgiveness visualization, available at http://www.newharbinger.com/45397.

Nina Remembers… *While teaching at a Buddhist retreat center in Massachusetts, we saw a sign on the main shrine room door. This profound wisdom stays with me:*

Let It Be. In the end, only three things matter:
how much you loved, how gently you lived,

*and how gracefully you let go of
what was
not meant for you.*
—*Buddha*

Journaling to Freedom

Write a letter to your former love partner or yourself. Forgive by proclaiming your release of painful feelings and relinquishment of retaliation. If you can't forgive right now, state it as you want it to be. Rewrite this letter as you need to.

Dear _____,

_____
_____
_____
_____
_____
_____
_____

Disentanglement opens the door for you to relate better with yourself. The next chapter on self-image will move you forward.

Action Steps for Moving Onward

As always, share with a trusted friend or support group.

1. Complete the exercises on how you remain entangled.

   a. Rate your abandonment, woundedness, and detachment issues.

   b. Take the assessment on specific ways you remain entangled.

2. Contemplate the When Your Disentanglement Is Complete visualization (downloadable audio). Write specific goals for when you've put your relationship loss behind you.

3. Write your good, bad, and ugly lists for your ended relationship. Add new items as they occur to you.

4. Change thoughts and feelings.

   a. Catalog entangling thoughts and feelings.

   b. Do mindfulness release.

   c. Reframe thoughts. Do more as other thoughts and emotions arise.

   d. Change interpretation of feelings with the emotional schema therapy technique.

5. Set boundaries in your thoughts, emotions, behavior, and interactions with your ex-partner.

a. List what you can use for "sad time" and "mad time." Use them for emotional release.

b. List feelings of remaining emotional attachment. If need be, make the list of how your ex-partner is not meeting your needs now.

c. Do "glad time" reinforcement of positive feelings.

d. Plan to release old memories by making new ones, creating new rituals, reconnecting with friends.

6. Listen to the Cutting Heartstrings visualization (downloadable audio). I recommend you have a supportive person with you when you work through these steps. You may need to go through this visualization more than once as you disentangle.

7. Listen to the Letting Go meditation (downloadable audio).

8. Contemplate the Appropriate Forgiveness visualization (downloadable

audio) at least three times this week. Write the forgiveness letter.

9. Nurture yourself. You deserve to acknowledge your courage in doing this work.

Part IV

Renewing Yourself

Divorce strikes hard at our belief in self and self-worth. It also tends to reopen lifelong wounds that impair all of our relationships, with self as well. The next four chapters approach these issues from different angles, giving you the insight, encouragement, and skills to help you express the essence of who you are—a valuable, lovable human being.

Chapter 11 looks into the origins of self-image and self-worth, exploring the question, "Who am I?"

Chapter 12 examines the evolution of identity: "How do I fit in?"

Chapter 13 explores the rewards of letting down masks and being authentically you: "How can I be the real me?"

Chapter 14 brings these discussions together in promoting

self-love: "How can I care for myself?"

Chapter 11

Raising Self-Worth by Changing Self-Image

We all carry it within us: supreme strength, the fullness of wisdom, unquenchable joy.
It is never thwarted and cannot be destroyed.
—Huston Smith

STEPS ALONG THE WAY

1. **The Ingredients of Self**
2. **Self-Image Development**
3. **How to Improve Your Self-Image**
4. **Obstacles to Changing Self-Image**

Divorce affects how you think and feel about yourself and how you see yourself in the world. At its core, it's a self-image issue. Therefore, recovery is based on your choices about self-image.

The Ingredients of Self

Many people use self-concept, self-image, and self-worth interchangeably, but they're not the same. Each has a separate meaning. Together, they frame your experience of life, create your relationship with self, and indicate how to make both more rewarding.

Self-Concept, Self-Image, and Self-Worth

Self-concept is based in the totality of your life experience: all you've seen, heard, touched, tasted, and smelled as well as all your thoughts, feelings, desires, and actions. This mass of experience is too unwieldy for everyday awareness. It's focused in *self-image*, the beliefs you have about yourself (Limón and Whalen 1986, 151).

Self-concept and self-image can be broken down into the following categories. (The descriptions that follow are representative, not a complete list.) Self-concept is *what you've experienced* in each category. Self-image is *what*

you think about yourself concerning the ingredients in each category.
1. *Character:* intelligence, sense of humor, assertiveness, choice-making.
2. *Physical care:* health habits and appearance.
3. *Community:* yourself as a friend, friends, activities shared.
4. *Economic:* education, career, use of financial resources.
5. *Relating:* sharing with self and others—physical (touch, sensuality, sexuality), intellectual (thoughts, fantasies), and emotional (feelings).
6. *Spiritual:* celebration of life, including religion, meditation, philosophy.
7. *Moral principles:* expressed through behavior—what you live for and would die for.

Self-image:
- Affects all experience by filtering perceptions, thoughts, feelings, desires, and behavior.
- Is dynamic. You activate different self-images with different people.

- Is difficult to evolve beyond the development of those around you. This applies to your family of origin as well as friends, love partners, and career relationships.

Self-worth (or self-esteem) is the direct consequence of self-image. How you think about yourself in each of the previous categories (self-image) creates a corresponding feeling (self-worth):
- When you validate yourself and feel effective at meeting your needs, this promotes high self-worth.
- When you believe you are ineffective at meeting needs and feel depressed or unhappy, this fosters low self-worth (Limón and Whalen 1986, 151).

Being mindful of the definitions above, pick an aspect of self-concept (life experiences) in the categories. (Do more as you can.) For each category, describe your corresponding self-image (beliefs about self) and feelings of self-worth that follow. Here's an example, showing two different sets of self-image and self-worth based on the same economic characteristic of education.

Aspect of self-concept: Graduated with master's degree in music. Teach at a junior college.

Person A:
Self-image: Positive. I am a good instructor for my students.
Self-worth: High. I feel good about myself in my career.

Person B:
Self-image: Negative. I wanted to teach at a university. I have not achieved my goal.
Self-worth: Low. I feel like a failure in my career.

Notice how both people define their worth by their behavior instead of their inherent goodness as a human being. More on this later.

1. Character: _____
_____

    Self-image: _____
    Self-worth: _____

2. Physical care: _____
_____

    Self-image: _____
    Self-worth: _____

3. Community: _____

   Self-image: _____
   Self-worth: _____
4. Economic: _____

   Self-image: _____
   Self-worth: _____
5. Relating: _____

   Self-image: _____
   Self-worth: _____
6. Spiritual: _____

   Self-image: _____
   Self-worth: _____
7. Moral principles: _____

   Self-image: _____
   Self-worth: _____

What stands out for you after looking at yourself this way? What areas do you most want to change?

_____
_____
_____

The Essential Self

The *essential self* is based on our fundamental worthiness as part of life. When free from emotional clutter and external demands, you may hear your essential self speaking in soft words of loving acceptance. Connecting with this deepest self brings great joy and peace. Following the guidance of this voice will lead you to a loving sense of "home" within yourself.

Interplay of Self-Concept, Self-Image, and Self-Worth; Their Relationship to the Essential Self

The following diagram correlates these concepts.

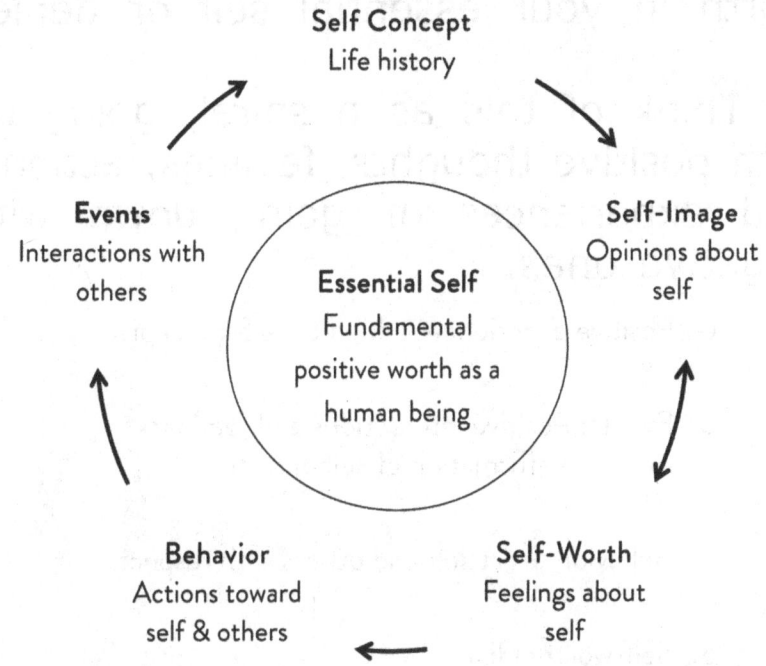

Correlations of Self-Concept, Self-Image, and Self-Worth to Essential Self

You experience life (self-concept) and give yourself a meaning within that experience (self-image), and this prompts an emotional response (self-worth). There's a rebound: self-worth can affect how you think about yourself (self-image). Also, self-worth affects your actions toward self and others (behavior), which affects interactions (events) and influences your life-experience (self-concept). This interplay either affirms your fundamental worth in your essential self or denies it.

Think of this as a spiral, going up with positive thoughts, feelings, actions, and experiences or going down with negative ones.

    6. Positive experiences added to self-concept.

    5. Events: Positive interactions and feedback reinforce affirmation of self and life.

    4. Behavior: Treat self and others with respect.

    3. Self-worth: High.

    2. Self-image: Affirming about self and life.

    1. Self-concept: Life experiences difficulties seen as opportunities for growth.

Self-Concept, Self-Image, Self-Worth Positive Spiral

1. Self-concept: Life experiences.
2. Self-image: Shaming about self and life.
3. Self-worth: Low.
4. Behavior: Treat self and others with disrespect, passively or aggressively, or shaming.
5. Events: Negative interactions and feedback from others reinforce shame or unhappiness.
6. Negative experiences added to self-concept.

Self-Concept, Self-Image, Self-Worth Negative Spiral

Divorce is a prime example of this spiral (as seen in chapter 10). Here's a more complete description. Consider the divorced person who views it as a totally negative experience:

1. *Self-concept:* Divorce as part of personal history.
2. *Self-image:* Divorce interpreted as failure to be good spouse or lover.
3. *Self-worth:* Low in intimacy, social, and values. This affects self-image and attitudes about appearance and personality, which pulls overall self-worth even lower.

4. *Behavior:* Diminished job performance threatens economic self-image.
5. *Events:* Ineffective work performance and social isolation cause missed promotion and alienation.

These become part of life history (self-concept) that get defined in self-image as confirmation of shortcomings, which lowers self-worth.

This illustrates the huge impact divorce has on one's life. Even though others may empathize, validate this individual's struggles, and enjoy his or her personality, unless this person changes self-image about divorce, self-worth will remain low and connection with the essential self will be difficult.

Here's a positive spiral:
1. *Self-concept:* Involvement in divorce-recovery seminar.
2. Self-image: Though difficult, with support and knowledge, grows from this experience. "I'm okay even though I'm getting a divorce."

3. Self-worth: High. Works through feelings of anger and grief. Emotions show capacity for love.
4. Behavior: Interaction in class: processing emotions and learning new skills. Becoming assertive with self and others.
5. *Events:* Readjustment brings new friendships and career goals.

These reaffirm positive self-image and high self-worth, building a strong connection to the essential self.

Simply trying to raise self-worth is the incorrect approach. The key areas for healthy change are self-image and behavior. Let's begin by understanding how negative upbringing influences the development of self-image and its effects in your current life and on your divorce. Then, we'll explore how to make positive change and consciously connect with your essential self.

Self-Image Development

Growing children define self-image and feel resulting self-worth from how parenting figures care for them. However, *regardless of childhood experiences, realize that you create who you are now.* A simple, profound concept of healthy development called the "five freedoms" will help you.

The Five Freedoms

We are all born with the potential to fulfill what Virginia Satir (1995) called the "five freedoms."

1. The freedom to see and hear what is there instead of what "should" be, was, or will be.
2. The freedom to say what you feel and think, instead of what you "should" feel and think.
3. The freedom to feel what you feel, instead of what you "ought" to feel.
4. The freedom to ask for what you want, instead of always waiting for permission.
5. The freedom to take risks on your own behalf, instead of choosing to be only "secure."

The following is my interpretation of these five freedoms correlated to the ingredients that comprise self-image and self-worth.

1. *Sense awareness.* The freedom to use your five natural senses: see, hear, touch, taste, and smell and accept this as your experience of the world. These are not necessarily what others sense or the way the world really is. This informs your *self-concept.*
2. *Thoughts.* The freedom to judge the information from your senses. Again, these are not necessarily reality. These include your opinions about yourself, your *self-image.*
3. *Feelings.* The freedom to have emotional responses from your judgments, including feelings about yourself, *self-worth.*
4. *Wants and needs.* The freedom to desire that things or people, self included, act in a certain way.
5. *Behavior choice.* The freedom to choose actions and be responsible for them.

Small children readily possess these freedoms:
1. *Sense awareness:* Easily share sensory experience as when something is "smelly."

2. Thoughts: Hilarious interpretations about life.
3. Feelings: Cry loudly or show anger.
4. Wants and needs: Children know what they want for Christmas.
5. *Behavior choice:* Without prior direction, children will readily choose what to do. Responsibility for consequences doesn't appear until older.

With healthy upbringing, we would've learned to use these five freedoms to build a positive self-image and high self-worth. What happened? Chapter 6, on damage control, introduced how toxic shame shackles one to a negative self-image and resulting low self-worth. This occurs in the abandonment of the child by parenting figures through the lack of healthy modeling and the active suppression or actual abuse of the child's physical, emotional, intellectual, and spiritual development. This causes the child to accept a self-image that he or she is fundamentally flawed as a human being.

The following childhood messages describe the impairment of the five freedoms by shame. Rate yourself on a scale of 1 (low) to 10 (high) for these effects on your five freedoms. Note the examples in the context of divorce.

Original Five Freedoms:	Sense Awareness	Thoughts	Feelings	Wants & Needs	Behavior Choice
Effects of Shame:	Non-Sense	False Self	Frozen Feelings	Lost Self	Masked Self

Which two freedoms had the highest rating of impairment? Why?

1. _____

2. _____

Your reactions: _____

The most revealing indicators of self-image are behaviors that either build self-worth or tear it down. Assess your involvement with these addictive-compulsive behaviors as indicators of poor self-image and low self-worth, and likely shame. (This is *not* meant for you to shame yourself. *Remember, what you do is not who you are, only an indicator of who you think you are.*) Most everyone can identify with some of these behaviors. Build motivation to change self-image and behaviors in ways that celebrate your fundamental worthiness. Rate yourself for past and present behavior on a scale of 0 (never) to 10 (frequent) incidence.

	Past	Present
1. Alcohol		
a. Misuse (avoid reality)		
b. Abuse (legal or physical problems)		
2. Drugs		
a. Misuse (avoid reality)		
b. Abuse (legal or physical problems)		
3. Food (overeating, undereating, diet pills, laxatives, and so on)		
4. Exercise		
a. Misuse (avoidance of problems)		
b. Abuse (destructive regimens)		
5. Thrill-seeking (undue risks)		
6. Workaholism		
7. Busyholism (activity to avoid feelings)		
8. Physical problems:		
a. Chronic health problems (stress-related)		
b. Sexual unresponsiveness (nonphysical cause)		
9. Smoking		
10. Violence (offender, repeat victim)		
11. Money use (compulsive shopping or gambling)		
12. Relationship problems		
a. Difficulty being intimate:		
i. Physically		
ii. Emotionally		
iii. Thoughts		
b. Difficulty keeping commitments (stuck in natural or adaptive child)		
c. Sex addiction (one-night stands, pornography)		
d. Overly controlling (stuck in critical parent)		
e. Overly dependent or codependent (stuck in nurturing parent)		
13. Entertainment (dependent on social media, internet, gaming, or TV to avoid reality, provide joy)		

Which three behaviors had the highest rating of impairment? Why?

1. _____
_____
2. _____
_____
3. _____
_____

How has this changed over time? _____
_____
_____

Your reaction: _____
_____

These assessments provide important information about the effects of shame in both your self-image and in your divorce process. Combine these with your previous assessments of childhood shame messages and low self-worth and shaming behaviors, and you get a clearer picture of the impact of shame in your life. Know that divorce is a tremendous opportunity to heal lifelong shame issues.

How to Improve Your Self-Image

It's time to move beyond who you've been in the past. The following are specific steps to improve your self-image as you deal with divorce and other traumatic events from the past: changing thoughts and changing behavior. (In chapter 13, on embracing your authenticity, we'll explore in greater detail how to heal the impact of shame to remove the false self.)

Changing Thoughts

Thought directs energy. What you think creates its own power. Choose what you want by dwelling on joy, self-confidence, love, wisdom, and so forth. Use these skills:

1. *Affirmations* are powerful ways to change self-image.

    a. Write a positive statement that you want to believe but do not at this time. Make it in the present tense: "I am..." rather than "I will..." Avoid negative words.

    b. Insert your name to make it personal and more powerful.

Examples: *I, Lisa, am lovable and capable just as I am. I, John, live life to the fullest. I, Carol, enjoy my career.*

c. Handwrite it thirty times per day for three weeks. This will probably take only ten minutes each day.

How do affirmations work? Look at Lisa. She suffers from low self-worth because her internal *critical parent* keeps reinforcing a self-image that she is worthless and dumb. When she starts writing her affirmation, "I, Lisa, am lovable and capable just as I am," this inner critic just repeats negative messages. Soon, the affirmation takes root through the power of repetition. Now, when confronted by a frustrating event, instead of self-criticisms, Lisa hears, "I, Lisa, am lovable and capable."

This leads her to believe in herself (changed self-image), have better feelings (increased self-worth), and reinforces successful behavior.

What three affirmations can you write?

1. _____

2. _____

3. _____

2. *Become an expert on what's strong.* Whenever you think of something you said or did that was a problem, think of something you've done that worked well. At the end of the day, make a list of what you accomplished. Concentrate on your successes. Unplug that internal machine that "talks you down." Learn from your mistakes, but don't dwell on them.

List qualities you admire in friends, family, and even in those you don't know (historical figures as well). Realize that you have some of that admired quality otherwise you wouldn't be able to recognize it in others (Limón and Whalen 1986).

Person	Positive Quality
1.	1.
2.	2.
3.	3.
4.	4.
5.	5.

3. *"Re-member" yourself.* Patrick O'Hara, the late codirector of the Growing Place, encouraged people to program themselves for success by saying, "I am now evolving—physically, mentally, emotionally, spiritually. My path is being opened before me, and I am going down it. Thank you for your help." Put energy forward rather than dwelling on old hurts.

Cultivate acceptance. Condemnation secures unhappiness. While you may not like that you're getting a divorce, learn to accept it as reality. Accept your natural fallibility as a human being. There's always the possibility of change. We may not always get what we want, but when we look for it, we always get what we need.

Separate your behavior from your person. When you make mistakes, don't shame yourself. *Evaluate your behavior so you can alter your actions to fit your positive self-worth rather than evaluating your worth by your behavior.*

Changing Behavior

Make changes in behavior by honoring the self and respectfully communicating that to others.

Determine your values, their priority, and live that way. Change your values to fit your behavior or change your behavior to fit your values. The gap in between is where unhappiness lurks.

Tell the truth. Telling the truth as you know it helps you live with integrity.

Create healthy environments. Have your home, work, and recreational environments be places of health, acceptance, and nurturing. Be with others who celebrate you, themselves, and life.

Listen and be of service to others. Interacting with others puts your problems into perspective and helps you get feedback so you can evaluate whether your intent is coming across.

Compliment people. This builds good connections, and it also reinforces your positive qualities. In addition, ask others how they developed this quality and learn their secrets for more effective living (Limón and Whalen 1986). Who can you compliment this week? (And they need not be profound, just simple gratitude.)

Person	Compliment
1.	1.
2.	2.
3.	3.
4.	4.
5.	5.

Cultivate positive habits and self-care. Proper diet, sleep, vocation, recreation, and spiritual practices are all essential to a positive self-image.

Create positive experiences. Become assertive; communicate effectively.

Obstacles to Changing Self-Image

The greatest difficulty of change is not the change itself but our attitudes. To change self-image, remove what blocks you. Start by examining which thoughts and behaviors are stumbling blocks. Rate yourself from 1 (low) to 10 (high). The antidotes are in italics.

1. "That's just the way I am!" You don't always have to be that way.	
2. "I'm afraid I'll make a bigger mistake!" You might make things better.	
3. "I'll never measure up." Compare who you are with you've been, not with others.	
4. "Maybe it will go away." Confronting issues ultimately lowers stress.	
a. Physical pain to mask emotional pain	
b. Thinking feelings away instead of experiencing them	
c. Replacing emotional hurt with distracting substance or behavior	
d. Dumping on yourself for having feelings that others or your inner critic disapproves of	
e. Taking inappropriate responsibility	
f. Avoiding the obvious and being blindsided	
g. Not taking any responsibility	
h. Maintaining social roles	
i. Criticizing others for their having feelings and thoughts your inner critic disapproves of	
5. "I don't know what to change!" Find out.	
6. "I don't know how to change!" Learn how.	
7. "Lord, make things better and do it now!" Patience gives you time to make best choices.	
8. "What? I've got to do it again?" Do what it takes.	
9. "But that's what I've always done!" Outer change requires inner change.	

What are your top three blocks? How do you propose to break through them?

1. Block: _____
How I'll break through: _____
2. Block: _____
How I'll break through: _____

3. Block: _____
How I'll break through: _____

Nina Remembers... *Bruce and I heard a proud New Zealander share how his difficult divorce had affected his self-esteem. This quote, often attributed to Sir Edmund Hillary, helped him rebuild: "It is not the mountain we conquer but ourselves."*

Being an expert on how you're stuck is only the beginning of the solution. Hopefully, it'll motivate you to overcome it. Your changes must be ones that make a difference.

Journaling to Freedom

Write a letter to your essential self. Invite its quiet voice into your mind and heart. Commit yourself to follow its guidance.

Dear Essential Self,

_____
_____
_____
_____
_____
_____
_____
_____

In chapter 13, on embracing your authenticity, we'll examine in greater depth the false self, those masks of shame that cloak the essential self. Until then, listen to the Analogies visualization (the downloadable audio is available at http://www.newharbinger.com/45397). The analogies are brief vignettes about self-image, self-worth, and healing from divorce. Let them take root in your mind and heart, and bear fruit.

Action Steps for Moving Onward

Share the results of these exercises with trusted others.

1. Explore the characteristics of your self-concept, self-image, and resulting self-worth.

2. Rate yourself on the effects of shame on the five freedoms. Discuss how these connect with shame issues from your childhood.

3. Take the assessment on shame-based behavior. Notice the differences and similarities of past behavior with that of the present. Discuss how you learned to do these. Make commitments to change.

4. Choose an affirmation and write it thirty times per day for the next three weeks.

5. List positive qualities you recognize in others (and therefore yourself).

6. List compliments to others. Express them and get others' wisdom about living.

7. Assess the obstacles to change. Determine how you might overcome them. Get others to help you brainstorm solutions.

8. Write your letter to your essential self.

9. Listen to the Analogies visualization (downloadable audio), which is about self-image and self-worth.

10. Listen to the My Life, My Choice meditation (downloadable audio).

11. Keep celebrating your healthy changes.

Chapter 12

Transition: Developing Identity

A man can only be young once, but he can be immature forever.
—Catherine Aird

STEPS ALONG THE WAY

1. **How You Became You**
2. **Exploring Your Identity Development**
3. **Reparenting Yourself**

Have you ever wondered why people behave the way they do: your aunt doing whatever your uncle says, your cousin finding a fight wherever he goes? What's behind your parents' behavior? How did you become you and choose your ex-partner? There are answers to these questions. They come from exploring identity.

While divorce is a major life transition, all life *is* change. You can either be pulled about or take charge.

Harness change by understanding how your identity formed and "reparenting" yourself to evolve your ability to relate. This chapter will show you the way.

How You Became You: A Theory of Identity Development

A theory of identity described in *Rebuilding: When Your Relationship Ends* has a simplicity that illuminates the process of becoming an individual and points the way toward continuing growth (Fisher and Alberti 2016). The original theory characterized the development of identity in three stages: shell, rebel, and love. These are ideal descriptions for the first two stages. I rename the third stage "loving-acceptance" to eliminate confusion with romantic love. I also divide the theory into a primary process and a secondary process.

The Primary Process

The primary process is the original tour through the three developmental stages. Some individuals never leave the primary process by remaining stuck

either in the shell or the rebel stage or both. For each stage, we'll explore:
1. Components of ideal development (ages can vary, those given are typical benchmarks). You will apply these descriptions to current relationships.
2. Being stuck in a particular stage and its effect on relationships.

Shell Stage

Age: Zero to eleven years old.

Identity: Dormant. The child's identity is incomplete. Healthy parenting helps the child grow into an assertive self. Excessive parental control can stifle identity development and foster repression or rebellion.

Attitude: "I should," conforming to rules at home and school.

Behavior: Passive. The child relies on parental figures to make decisions and choices. This diminishes as children grow older.

Relationships: Stable. Communication is one-way, from parent to child. The relationship is balanced where the child is dependent upon others to meet needs while seeking to please others.

Are there current relationships in your life where you are in the shell stage? _____

_____

_____

Rebel Stage

The rebel stage initiates the search for identity. This stage is divided into external and internal rebellion. Both can occur at any age.

External Rebellion

Age: "Typical" adolescence runs from twelve to eighteen.

Identity: Seeking identity. An adolescent's attempts to establish individuality create inevitable conflicts. The motivation is positive even if specific behavior causes difficulties. The end result of external rebellion is a unique sense of self, an identity. Some teenagers go in destructive directions: theft, joining gangs, or taking drugs. Others become "aginers" by being against everybody else. Many find self through involvement in academics, sports, drama, music, or other appropriate pursuits.

Attitude: "I won't!" The individual pushes limits to find the self. Limits are important for a person in the rebel stage. It's also a time of increased independence: "I want to do it myself!" This builds emotional strength and self-confidence.

Behavior: Aggressive or passive-aggressive. The drive for independence often appears in irresponsible behavior. Curiously, this is reinforced by shell-stage conformance to a peer group. Rule-questioning can be constructive, for example the adolescent who becomes the first in the family to go to college. *Rebellion need not be "revolting." It means change.*

Relationships: Unstable. Conflicts bring up unresolved adolescent issues in parents. With awareness, this can be a time of tremendous growth for all.

Are there current relationships in which you are in external rebellion? _____
_____
_____

Will's Take *Setting limits reminds me of a spider plant I repotted. Although I fed it, watered it, and sang to it, the plant still wouldn't grow. Later, I learned that the root system needed to reach the sides of the bigger pot before the upper plant would grow. In the same way, someone in rebellion needs to push against limits to develop.*

Internal Rebellion

Internal rebellion is dissatisfaction with an area of life coupled with the drive to change it. Adolescents seek identity driven by internal rebellion. Without appropriate limits, modeling, and instruction, they tend to turn outward and push at others (parents, teachers, "society") in external rebellion rather than turn inward to develop their uniqueness. The same is true for the grown-up rebel during divorce who may have affairs or overspend to feel better, all the while blaming his or her partner.

Rebellion acted out externally by blaming others doesn't resolve the desire for growth; it only masks it. Internal rebellion is a positive force when we take responsibility and change appropriately.

Here are the positive aspects of internal rebellion.

Age: It can occur whenever there is a desire for change.

Identity: Seeking identity internally leads to gaining a better sense of self. This results from self-responsibility.

Attitude: "I will!" Ownership to make the desired changes establishes a balance within oneself and one's life.

Behavior: Assertive with self, an essential step to being assertive with others.

Relationships: Less conflict because self-responsible people understand that positive growth lies in evolving oneself.

Positive internal rebellion is the drive for responsible change. It alternates with the loving-acceptance stage within adults who realize that life is a cycle of growth and stabilization.

Are there areas of your life where you are in internal rebellion? _____
_____

Loving-Acceptance Stage

The loving-acceptance stage is a time for consolidation. The "shoulds" of the shell stage are gone. The "I won't" of external rebellion has been replaced with the "I will" of responsible internal rebellion. This brings healthier, happier, more satisfying relationships both with self and others. Unfortunately, many people never reach this stage.

> *Age:* Psychological and emotional maturity can occur as early as the middle teens.
>
> *Identity:* Secure. Basic regard and acceptance of self is solid. Changes in career and relationship reinforce an identity of worthiness. This individual is strong enough to accept others for who they are and not try to change them.
>
> *Attitude:* "I choose," two powerful words that describe

self-responsibility. Mature self-love is foundational for mature love and compassion for others.

Behavior: Assertive with respectful actions that reflect values.

Relationships: Cooperative. Two-way communicating takes both partners' needs into account and involves active listening. Conflicts are resolved appropriately.

Are there current relationships in your life where you are in loving acceptance?

_____

_____

_____

Listen to the Loving-Acceptance Stage visualization (available at http://www.newharbinger.com/45397) to find comfort and familiarity with this stage. Return to it whenever you find the need to reinforce its message. Though you may still harbor feelings of grief, anger, shame, and abandonment toward others, in this visualization, allow yourself to feel your emotions but don't get stuck in them. Imagine yourself flowing beyond them into loving acceptance.

This acceptance does not mean that you approve of others' behavior. Rather, it's your willingness to let go of attempts to make others change. You may need to go through this visualization many times to accomplish this. As you find yourself growing into the loving-acceptance stage, you'll be taking giant steps toward health and freedom in your life.

Many have asked, "Can I go from shell stage straight to the loving-acceptance stage without rebelling?" The answer is no because you cannot fully accept something unless you've given yourself the option to reject it. Even if you choose the same behavior in your loving-acceptance stage that you did in your shell stage, the time of questioning, however brief, is a rebel-stage action.

Complications Within the Developmental Theory

1. When parents remain stuck in the shell stage, it's difficult for their children to grow out of it without the positive influence from other, more mature, authority figures. Rebellion in the child can be very

unstable when parents themselves have not completed their own rebel stage.
2. Without appropriate limits from healthy parental guidance, it's difficult to get the emotional strength to grow out of the shell stage.

Grown-Up Relationships

Just as individuals can become stuck in particular TA ego states, many grown-ups remain stuck in the shell or external-rebel stage. These people don't reach the full maturity of positive internal rebellion and the loving-acceptance stages. Like overgrown children or adolescents, they go through life in unhealthy dependent or codependent relationships or suffer as loners. The grown-up who is stuck in shell stage or external-rebellion stage relates in the following manner. This is contrasted with the loving-acceptance stage.

Shell stage. Though the shell stage is necessary for early growth, problems occur when individuals stay in its protected cocoon. Their relationships remain stagnant.

Parents: Relates toward parents as if he or she were still their child because he or she "should." Examples: The man who takes a job to please Mom, the woman who only buys cars approved of by Dad.

Friends: Does what everyone else does. Disagreement and conflict are avoided to prevent abandonment by the group.

Love partner: Becomes involved in relationships of immature dependence or codependence because identities were never discovered. Shell-stage people who feel threatened by changes in their love partner can become controlling through verbal or physical abuse. They cling to the other person because they cannot face rejection and abandonment.

Working relationships: Lets the company care for them just as their parents did. Corporate downsizing is most threatening.

TA ego states. Three ego states, each with the common denominator of dependence:
- Natural child: "Please take care of me so I'll be okay or so I can be irresponsible."
- Nurturing parent: "Let me take care of you so you won't abandon me."
- Critical parent: Dependency is two-fold: subordinate to rules and a penchant for control makes this person dependent on relationships with others who can be controlled.

Will's Take *Barry, a forty-seven-year-old man, said in a shocked tone, "I've been in the shell stage my whole life." Remember, psychological and emotional maturity is up to you.*

External rebellion. The rebel pushes against others as if they were his or her parent.
- *Parents:* Acts like a rebellious teenager with parents.
- *Friends:* Often destroys friendships. The rebel may become a loner for a time, or bounce around, seeking to belong.

Love partner: Acts like irresponsible teenager, rebelling against love partner: affairs, verbal or physical abuse, or silence and physical remoteness. Unless a person matures, he or she tends to become like one parent and marry someone like the other parent.

Working relationships: Pushes against boss, is insubordinate, or continually shows up late for work and gets fired. Person may job-hop.

TA ego states: Natural child and adaptive child. Both are irresponsible. The natural child changes jobs and relationships like an overgrown kid, looking for fun. The adaptive child manipulates and blames: "You're causing all the problems because you're like your mother!"

Loving-acceptance stage. The people who evolve into this stage have many rewards. Chief among them are healthy relationships.

Parents: Behaves respectfully and lovingly toward parents while assertively setting appropriate boundaries.

Friends: Loving give and take. Conflict dealt with appropriately.

Love partner: The most desirable love relationship: a deepening friendship combined with nourishing sexual intimacies. Both partners are givers and receivers. Dedication is threefold: to self, partner, and the relationship.

Working relationships: Assertive, respectful with integrity.

TA ego state: Adult. Flexibly determines how best to meet internal needs (parent-part and child-part) in the context of a social world. The adult compromises with care, forethought, and cooperation guided by values and morality.

Where are you in your current grown-up relationships (what stages and ego states)?

Parents: _____

Friends: _____

Love relationships: _____

Working relationships: _____

Your reactions: _____

The divorce-recovery process is a catalyst for you to move through the shell and rebel stages into the loving-acceptance stage. After divorce, the person who remains stuck in the shell stage is likely to ineffectively retreat to parents for protection or seek another shell-stage partner to maintain a sense of security. The individual who continues to be stuck in the rebel stage may drift from partner to partner or fight endless court battles over money, kids, and possessions. The person who grows into the loving-acceptance stage assertively deals with legalities and builds positive friendships while consciously healing divorce wounds.

The Secondary Process

In the loving-acceptance stage, change is celebrated as part of life. Just as someone in the adult ego state appropriately attends to needs of the child and parent ego states, a person in the loving-acceptance stage appropriately applies shell-stage and rebel-stage behaviors and attitudes in specific contexts. I call this the *secondary process.*

Take Cynthia, who has become dissatisfied with her job. Someone stuck in the shell stage would stay in the job purely for security. An external rebel would demand changes at work or quit the job abruptly and thereby create even greater problems. Coming from the loving-acceptance stage, Cynthia's need for change (internal rebellion) helps her examine options and act on a new decision appropriately: return to college. This behavior brings radical change. Yet managed by her adult, this rebellion is appropriate. Once in the classroom, Cynthia takes on a shell-stage aspect of being a student, subordinate to the greater knowledge of the instructor(s). This does not mean that she's passive. Assertive questioning, dialog, and research is essential to academic training. Both this internal rebel stage–centered behavior and shell-stage posture fit appropriately into her overall loving-acceptance stage personality.

Where in your life are you in secondary rebellion? _____

Exploring Your Identity Development

As with any theory, application of actual data helps make it real. Before you examine your life experiences, let's look at an example to guide you. Jill is a fifty-five-year-old woman. Here are timelines of her life:

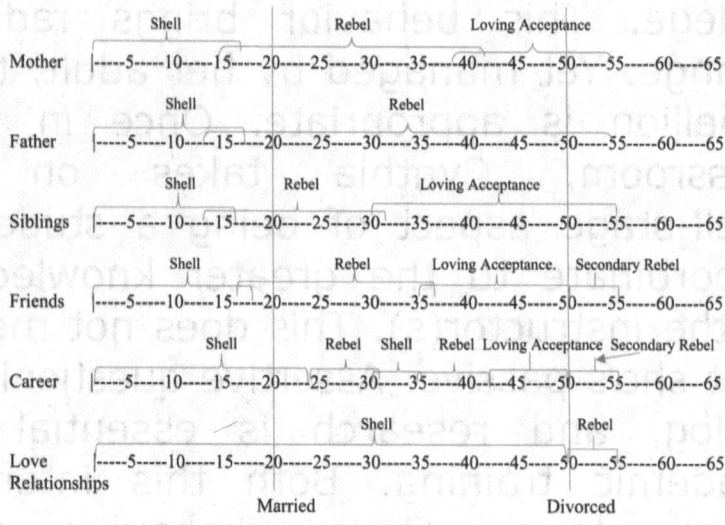

Jill's Timelines

Through Jill's timelines, you can see the length of each stage and the ages in which Jill transitioned from one stage to another. (Note: Some stages overlap others.) Here's a summary to evaluate what Jill needs to do to reparent herself.

1. Jill has reached the loving-acceptance stage with her mother, siblings, friends, and in her career.
2. Jill is still in rebellion with her father. She's also in rebellion in her love relationships.
3. In her career, Jill has bounced back and forth between shell and rebel, finally landing in loving-acceptance. She's now in secondary stage rebellion, training for a new position.
4. Note that Jill got married when she was in external rebellion in all areas of her life except for love relationships. There, she was in the shell stage. She had been in college and dropped out to marry her husband, leaving her family and friends behind.

5. Jill was a dumpee at age fifty. This kicked her into primary rebellion in her love-relationships and secondary rebellion in her career and with friends. This occurred when she moved from her town to a different city to train for her new position and built a new friendship network.

Reparenting. Jill needs to continue her growth as an individual and a love-partner to reach loving acceptance. Her relationship with her father also needs development to reach the loving-acceptance stage.

To lay out your life in this fashion, make it simple. Go through the timelines one at a time.

1. Bracket the length of time you were in each stage—shell stage, rebel stage (external), loving-acceptance—in the following relationships. If you find that you've completed the primary process in any relationship, note where you engaged in a secondary process.

2. When you've finished, draw a vertical line through all the timelines:
    a. For when you committed to your ex-love partner.
    b. For when your love relationship ended.
3. Answer the questions at the end.

Doing your timelines may not be easy. However, it will enable you to identify where you need to reparent yourself, evolve your identity, and build healthier relationships beyond divorce recovery.

Mother	---5----10----15---20---25---30---35---40---45---50---55---60---65---
Father	---5----10----15---20---25---30---35---40---45---50---55---60---65---
Siblings	---5----10----15---20---25---30---35---40---45---50---55---60---65---
Friends	---5----10----15---20---25---30---35---40---45---50---55---60---65---
Career	---5----10----15---20---25---30---35---40---45---50---55---60---65---
Love relationships	---5----10----15---20---25---30---35---40---45---50---55---60---65---

1. Are you still in the original shell stage? With whom? _____
    How do you act with that person(s)? _____

2. Are you still in the original rebel stage? With whom? _____
How do you act with that person(s)? _____
_____
_____

How much is external rebellion? _____
How much is internal rebellion? _____

3. Are you in the loving-acceptance stage? With whom? _____
How do you act with that person(s)? _____
_____
_____

4. Have you reached the secondary process? With whom? _____
How do you act with that person(s)? _____
_____
_____

5. What stages were you in for all relationships when you entered into your now-ended love relationship?
_____
_____

6. What stages were you in for all relationships when you ended your love relationship?

_____

_____

7. What do these last two questions tell you about why you chose your ex-partner?

_____

_____

8. What do you think you must do to reparent yourself and make better choices in the future?

_____

_____

Reparenting Yourself

You may well ask, "Well, *how* do I reparent myself and get to the loving-acceptance stage?" The skills and approaches in this workbook all help you learn what you didn't get growing up:

1. Getting in touch with your emotions and expressing them appropriately.
2. Establishing your adult ego state.
3. Becoming assertive.
4. Overcoming shame as you raise self-worth through changed self-image.
5. Fostering self-love as you establish loving acceptance for yourself.

These approaches build a better understanding of others so you can connect in more authentic, loving ways. This is the promise in the pain of divorce: your development as a loving human being.

Journaling to Freedom

Write a letter to proclaim your developing self: your strengths, your patience to be an accepting person, and your willingness to care for yourself by setting healthy boundaries and releasing demands that others change.

_____
_____
_____
_____
_____
_____
_____
_____

The next chapter will continue identity development by helping you open up to authenticity.

Action Steps for Moving Onward

1. Answer the questions after each stage description.

2. Mark the timelines and answer the questions that follow. Discuss answers with a trusted friend or family member.

3. Make healthy changes (positive rebellion): start an exercise or diet program, join a club, develop a new interest or hobby.

4. Listen to the Loving-Acceptance Stage visualization (downloadable audio) at least three times this week.

5. Listen to the Growing Older, Getting Smarter meditation (downloadable audio).

6. Write the letter to yourself about your strengths, patience, self-care, and acceptance of others.

7. Continue nurturing yourself for your efforts on this healing journey.

Chapter 13

Openness: Embracing Authenticity

If you can't be yourself, what's the point of being anyone else?
—Tennessee Williams

STEPS ALONG THE WAY

1. **The False Self and Masks of Deception**
2. **The Games of Masks**
3. **Letting Go of the False Self**

Recovery from relationship loss provides many lessons, none more important than becoming authentic with self and others. *Authenticity starts with embracing the positive worth that always resides in you.* To accomplish this, you must remove the toxic shame barriers between your everyday self and your essential self. These barriers, "false-self" beliefs in fundamental defectiveness (described in chapter 11), construct a negative self-image maintained through masks. You may be tempted to keep wearing masks because they seem to reduce conflict as many people in your life are accustomed to your false selves. However, removing them is worth it because you'll reclaim your birthright of beauty, worth, and spiritual connection and find the most important love relationship: the one with you.

Let's start by defining masks and how they represent the false self both generally and during divorce. Next, we'll look at the role of shame in the development of the false self and the use of masks. Then, we'll break through to the real you.

The False Self and Masks of Deception

Though we all desire acceptance and love, many people believe in a shame-based self-image, which prompts fears:
- I'm not worthy of love.

- If you really knew me, you'd reject me, so I must hide my true thoughts and feelings.
- If you rejected me, I'd be alone for the rest of my life.

Individuals try to reduce fear by wearing masks to conceal the shame-based self-image, acting in ways they believe others will accept. These fears are reinforced during divorce. Without healing, one may carry these masks into future relationships and sabotage intimacy.

Will's Take *Anna said she wore a mask throughout her marriage, and then her husband left. "I would rather have been 'dumped' as my real self than the way it is now, not knowing if I would've been accepted." Stuart remarked, "I don't wear any masks." But after discussion, he said, "Why, all I am are masks. Who is the real me?"*

The use of masks can be appropriate, for example when a stranger asks how you are, you'd be quite correct to say, "Fine," regardless of how you really feel. Social banter consists of such pleasantries.

Be honest with yourself to decide whether a mask is appropriate: "Is it best to share my true self with this person at this time?" Take into account your needs, those of others as you know them, and the situation. Here, shame is an obstacle to conscious decision making because it blocks awareness of the inner self and renders self-honesty impossible.

These steps will help you make conscious, healthy decisions:
1. Understanding the concept of masks, when they are appropriate, and when not.
2. Evaluating your masks to discard those that represent a false self.
3. Reacquiring the five freedoms to embrace your essential self.

The concept of masks can also help you understand what happened in your ended relationship and learn how you may have contributed to the lack of intimacy.

Masks

Masks are powerful. We wear inappropriate masks at a very high cost. They make communication unhealthy, relationships counterfeit, and impair physical health. Most profoundly, they make our lives into an illusion as we deny our true selves. The question is: Do we control the mask, or does it control us? Since masks have an appropriate use, how can you determine when one is appropriate and at what times? Let's understand their types.

The External Mask

The external mask is used to portray your public self (outward behavior) in such a way as to hide your private self (thoughts, feelings, desires). It's appropriate or inappropriate use is illustrated by the following example.

While waiting for the divorce decree, Pat feels emotional pain but knows it wouldn't be appropriate to share it at work. So, Pat puts on an "I'm okay" external mask." A customer asks, "How are you today?" Pat replies, "Fine," and smiles. It's exhausting, but it helps Pat cope. The appropriate external mask is shown in the image below.

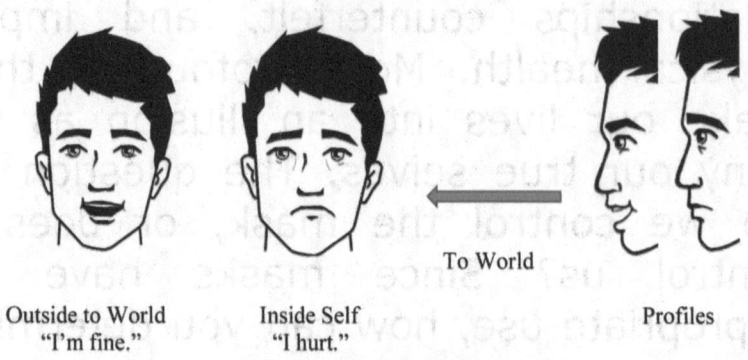

External Masks

One day, a good friend who lives out of town meets Pat for coffee to catch up. The friend asks Pat how things are going. Pat says, "Fine," and smiles just like at work. Instantly, the same external mask is now inappropriate. This friend is someone with whom Pat can honestly share. By hiding behind the "I'm okay" mask, Pat blocks emotional support.

Later, Pat goes home feeling even more lonely and depressed. Where Pat found solace at work by hiding feelings from others, the inappropriate use of this external mask with the friend cost Pat a supportive connection. This demonstrates how intimacy is blocked when we aren't authentic.

The Internal Mask

An inappropriate internal mask creates the most problems because it often goes unrecognized. A negative internal mask rooted in the shame-based self-image of fundamental defectiveness hides the worthy private self from one's awareness. An alternate ending to the previous situation shows how this happens.

When Pat says, "I'm fine," the friend sees rings under Pat's eyes and notices heaviness in Pat's voice. "You say you're fine," says the friend, "but you look tired or anxious. Is something wrong? I want to help if I can." This invitation encourages Pat to let down the "I'm okay" external mask, and Pat says, "Things aren't fine. I'm separated, and we're going to get a divorce. I really hurt." Here, Pat shares authentically. Pat goes on, "I feel awful that I couldn't make my marriage work. I got counseling, and I tried to get my spouse to see a counselor, but nothing I tried helped."

Now, Pat's negative internal mask emerges when Pat says, "I'm such a failure."

Whoa! Can you see the difference between the authentic statement, "I really hurt," because of the divorce and the negative internal mask of "I'm such a failure"? Pat's negative internal mask is a false-self definition that Pat is a bad person because of the divorce. This negative internal mask can be represented as shown in the image below.

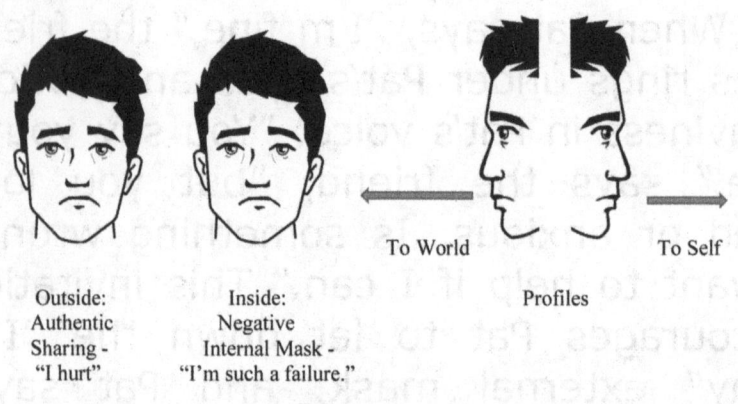

Internal Masks

Pat's friend may say, "Wait. It sounds like you did your best to save your marriage. It takes two to make it work. Don't blame yourself for everything." However, regardless of how supportive Pat's friend tries to be, if Pat continues to wear a negative internal mask, Pat will continue to feel shame about self because of the divorce.

This negative self-appraisal is a mask because Pat's definition of self is based on behavior, not on the fundamental goodness that's at everyone's core. If Pat's self-image stays constructed of shame-based negative internal masks, low self-esteem, a sense of hopelessness, and depression will result because these masks alienate one from self and others.

To remove a negative internal mask, cover it with a positive internal mask. This is done through the practice of affirmations: short, positive statements that you're attempting to believe. (See the discussion of affirmations in chapter 11.) When incorporated as a replacement view of self, the affirmation melts away the negative internal mask and leaves you with your positive authentic self.

Here's how this would work for Pat:
1. Pat identifies the negative internal mask: "I'm such a failure."
2. Pat selects an affirmation: "I, Pat, am lovable and capable just as I am." Pat writes this affirmation thirty times per day for three

weeks, puts notes up around the house, records it, and listens to the recording.
3. After some time (typically three weeks), Pat finds that the negative internal mask has melted away and realizes two things: (1) Pat is lovable and capable, and (2) it still hurts to go through divorce: "I'm okay even though I'm getting a divorce."

Let me be clear. Releasing shame from divorce isn't an easy process. It won't happen overnight. Going through divorce may open the door to lifelong shame issues, and counseling may be necessary to help you heal. Nevertheless, taking the actions outlined here will be a guiding light in your efforts to recover from divorce and other issues because discarding inappropriate external masks and negative internal masks is the leading edge of removing shame from your self-image. This helps you accept reality, even if painful, and to take steps to become the master of your life.

The Games of Masks

People hide their true selves in many ways. When individuals wear inappropriate external masks to avoid sharing honestly with others and negative internal masks to suppress awareness of their worthy private self, life becomes a series of games. John Powell (1999) described masks as "human hiding places." Here are examples drawn from Powell's work and Rebuilding Seminar participants (not a complete list). Notice how the core feelings of positive self-worth are suppressed under each shaming internal mask. The internal and external masks are generic. Space is provided for your own examples. What are your games of masks?

1. Overdeveloping one trait to counteract an opposite, unacceptable trait.

    a. *"I'm no good and feel bad about it"* feels low self-worth, overcompensates by being aggressive (to disprove inferiority) or passive (to withdraw from possible failure and guilt).

Sometimes feels inferior due to feeling guilty, and vice versa.

External mask: "Just watch me!" (fending off inferiority) "Watch me screw it up worse than anyone!" (inferior and guilty)

Shaming internal mask: "Don't watch me!" (guilty and inferior)

b. *Drama king or queen* needs turmoil to feel alive; submerges real self by creating crises, sabotaging serenity and intimacy.

External mask: "My life is exciting, therefore meaningful."

Shaming internal mask: "My life is meaningless."

c. *Stuck in my head* studies life rather than experiences it.

External mask: "I'm above it all, so I know what's best."

Shaming internal mask: "I can't cope with feelings."

d. *Comedian* escapes exposure of self through humor.

External mask: "Look how funny I am!"

Shaming internal mask: "I'm unworthy and unacceptable."

    e. *Macho man or woman* acts tough to have identity and worth. This precludes the vulnerability necessary for intimacy.

    External mask: "I can take it."

    Shaming internal mask: "I'm weak and can't be close."

2. Acting out because it's too threatening to be real.

    a. *Angerholic* throws rage around to distance others from his or her vulnerability. External mask: "Everything pisses me off!" Shaming internal mask: "I can't be vulnerable and share my real emotions."

    b. *All by myself* avoids life or relationships out of fear of inferiority. External mask: "I don't need anybody." Shaming internal mask: "No one wants me; I'm not lovable."

3. Attributing to others the unacceptable parts of oneself.

    a. *Cynic* believes the worst so there are no disappointments. Avoids dealing with reality. External mask: "Life's a bitch, and then you die." Shaming internal mask: "My life's a bitch until I die."

   b. *Poor little me* believes others conspire to attack. Suffering or complaining is the only response. External mask: "Everyone uses me." Shaming internal mask: "No one loves me because I'm unlovable."

4. Taking on the characteristics of another person, group, or role.

   a. *Big heart* takes care of others to the detriment of self, classic nurturing parent. External mask: "Here, let me care for you." Shaming internal mask: "I'm no good unless I give to others."

   b. *Hero* hides true desires behind roles. External mask: "I'll save you." Shaming internal mask: "I'll never be worth saving."

   c. *Chameleon* is the ultimate mask. Fits into every situation except being one's real self. External mask: "You'll always like me." Shaming internal mask: "I don't know me, and you shouldn't, either."

5. "Thinking" away feelings or justifying by any means that which is reprehensible.

   a. *Controller* has the need to dominate others to cover up suspected inadequacy in self (critical parent).

   External mask: "I know better than you."

   Shaming internal mask: "I don't know much at all."

   b. *"I'm fine"* hides from others in order to be acceptable by not rocking the boat.

   External mask: "I've got no problems."

   Shaming internal mask: "If you knew the real me, you wouldn't like me."

   c. *Breakable* believes it's too hard to cope with life and manipulates others into doing the "dirty work," overly sensitive, covertly controlling (adaptive child).

   External mask: "You must take care of me because I'm weak."

   Shaming internal mask: "I'm no good and can't make it on my own."

d. *Peacemaker* wants "peace at any price" because conflict is too painful. Without resolution of conflict, intimacy is avoided.

External mask: "Whatever you want."

Shaming internal mask: "My real wants and needs are unacceptable."

What masks do you wear? Give internal and corresponding external masks. Remember, rigorous honesty brings authenticity. Consider the masks you use with different individuals: ex-partner, family, coworkers, friends, dating partners. The inappropriate external mask is the leading edge of how shame affects your sense of self and enjoyment of life. The negative internal mask blocks connection with your essential self. Whether you start from the inside or the outside, this process is a pathway to authenticity.

External	Internal
1.	
a. With whom?	
b. Why?	
2.	
a. With whom?	
b. Why?	
3.	
a. With whom?	
b. Why?	
4.	
a. With whom?	
b. Why?	
5.	
a. With whom?	
b. Why?	

Your reactions: _____

When you reconnect with the inner self who may have been shamed, you reestablish the internal intimacy necessary for healing from divorce and creating a healthier life. Recognize your power to manage masks. Listen to the Unmasking Yourself visualization (available at http://www.newharbinger.com/45397) for each of the masks you described. Return to this visualization whenever you discover an inappropriate external or internal mask you want to remove.

Letting Go of the False Self

Regain awareness of your essential self by removing the barriers of shame. Then, establish a public self that portrays the healthy thoughts, feelings, wants, and needs of this essential self. Many fine books discuss this process (see Bradshaw 2005). Here, we can only give the broad outlines as it relates to divorce recovery. The assistance of a counselor or group can be most helpful.

Recovery of the Five Freedoms

Recall the five freedoms and the effect of shame upon them as outlined in chapter 11:

Original Five Freedoms:	Sense Awareness	Thoughts	Feelings	Wants & Needs	Behavior Choice
Effects of Shame:	Non-Sense	False Self	Frozen Feelings	Lost Self	Masked Self

Recovery begins when an individual realizes that life has become unmanageable and that pain produced by repeated addictive or compulsive behavior is greater than any temporary relief. Alcoholism, gambling, overeating, or getting in relationships to save you have only made life more complicated, frustrating, and miserable: drinking brought job loss, gambling depleted finances, overeating threatened health, and new love relationships soured into pain.

The decision to stop the addiction or compulsion and deal with life without distraction is the essential commitment to recovery. Examples:

- The spouse who voluntarily enters alcohol treatment.
- Faced with losing children because of abusive lovers, the single parent who goes to a safe house.
- The divorcing person gets therapy when stress causes illness.

Divorce is a catalyst for your conversion experience to choose health. Becoming responsible for yourself is where true recovery occurs.

Healthy Change Through Responsibility

Here, one regains the five freedoms or acquires their full use for the first time.

| Healthy Responsibility: | Open to the World | Transforming Thoughts | Freeing All Feelings | Integration of Wants & Needs | Living Consciously |

Mature responsibility requires a complete removal of inappropriate masks. Assess how much in your divorce recovery you have regained the five freedoms through healthy responsibility. Rate on a scale of 1 (low) to 10 (high).

1. *Open to the world.* Numbness is gone. You notice colors, temperatures, and sounds with greater sensitivity. Food tastes better; odors are more pungent. You feel reawakened.	Rating: _____
2. *Transforming thoughts.* You choose your interpretations instead of following others' judgments. You're able to understand and accept your part in relationship loss, not taking all responsibility or blaming your ex-partner. You set boundaries so others' opinions of you and the divorce do not unduly affect your positive view of self.	Rating: _____
3. *Freeing all feelings.* You feel relief from your loss and express and manage your emotions appropriately. You release shame and hurt from childhood abandonments that divorce brought up.	Rating: _____
4. *Integration of wants and needs.* You fulfill needs and choose wants. You deal forthrightly with divorce issues. Relationships are grounded in reality without avoidance or dwelling on divorce. You learn from this loss to live a better life.	Rating: _____
5. *Living consciously.* You bring the awareness of your inner self to your interactions with others. You have few leftovers about the divorce. You respond in the moment to situations rather than reacting to them hours or days later. You express thoughts, feelings, wants, and needs in actions that respect yourself and others.	Rating: _____

Which are higher? _____

What needs work? _____

Your reactions: _____

True recovery is a lifelong commitment to stop shaming yourself, enhance self-esteem, and prevent others

from ever shaming you again. As you heal from divorce and earlier difficulties, you become skilled at recognizing what's healthy and what's not. *Difficult choices must be made because you will frame wants and needs to fit into your chosen healthy self-image.* This may mean:
- Limiting attendance at family gatherings
- Getting counseling
- Ending unhealthy friendships
- Terminating unsatisfactory employment or changing careers.

Employ all five freedoms in the Embracing Yourself visualization (downloadable audio) to integrate those parts of yourself that you had hidden, either behind an external mask, internal mask, or both. Repeat as needed. With a stronger, more authentic self, you integrate these hurting selves into your greater essential self to be whole once again, free from the condemnation of shame.

Nina Remembers... *A Jungian therapist recalled Carl Jung's words, which were his daily reminder to be brave, drop masks, and choose the authenticity to be himself, no matter* *what: "The privilege of a lifetime is to become who you truly are."*

Journaling to Freedom

Write a letter from your essential self to your hurting selves who have worn inappropriate masks. Express the love of this deepest part of you. Share your commitment to care for yourself and live authentically.

Dear Hurting Selves,

_____
_____
_____
_____
_____
_____
_____
_____

Let go of old ways of being to make room for new ways of living. As the anonymous author of this quote so eloquently expresses:

Moving on involves the art of release—

learning to let go of old, dying selves;

of ideas that have reigned over us and had their day.

Release is to surrender securities no

longer valid—welcoming new visions,

emotions, and prospects.

When you connect with your essential self and embrace authenticity, new pathways open to uncover self-love. This sets the stage for healthier, loving relationships with others. The next chapter will help you.

Action Steps for Moving Onward

Share with a trusted friend or support group.

1. Assess your games of masks. Determine which masks you wear the most and reveal them in the Unmasking Yourself visualization (downloadable audio).

2. Assess your regaining of the five freedoms through healthy responsibility. Determine how you're growing into healthy use of the five freedoms as you take responsibility

for your divorce process and life after divorce.

3. Contemplate the Embracing Yourself visualization (downloadable audio) at least three times this week.

4. Write your letter to your hurting selves.

5. Celebrate your growth by connecting with nature: hiking, skiing, biking, gardening, or simply taking a walk. Use your five natural senses to experience these to the fullest.

Chapter 14

Uncovering Self-Love

Love is not at first anything that can be called merging or surrender or union with another....
It is an exalted occasion for the individual to ripen, to become something in himself [or herself].
—Rainer Maria Rilke, Letters to a Young Poet, translated by K.W. Maurer

STEPS ALONG THE WAY

1. **Experiencing Self-Love**
2. **Self-Love and Relationship Loss**
3. **The Committed Behavior of Self-Love**

Divorce recovery is a journey about love—the love you thought you had and perhaps did but not now, the love you still desire that may seem unattainable. For many people, love appears fleeting at best or only the words in songs and stories as if love is something to be found *out there*. However, the real nature of love is its timeless presence *inside* each of us. To bring love into your life, begin by uncovering love within yourself.

Experiencing Self-Love

It's natural to look outward for love. When we were children, parenting figures provided our basic physical, emotional, and psychological needs. They taught us ways to feel and express love, including self-love.

When children receive approval from parents for sharing physical affection, their feelings, and their thoughts and ideas, they build trust in themselves and in others. This fosters self-confidence and promotes positive self-image, self-esteem, and self-love. Healthy individuals learn to love the self just as much as they seek to love and be loved by others. Self-love is at the core of self-worth and assists us in maintaining healthy boundaries so we won't tolerate harmful relationships or make inappropriate demands.

Those children who are shamed, either through active abandonment or lack of healthy role modeling, may become deficient both in loving others and in loving themselves. This can produce grown-ups who go from one extreme (the needy, codependent lover who continually looks for others to provide the love and safety that was missing in childhood) to the other extreme (the fiercely independent person whose love and trust of self and others is so low that no one is allowed to get close).

However you were raised and whatever you learned, now is the time to cradle your life in your hands with the love you deserve and only you can give.

The Self-Love Process

In his excellent book *Learning to Love Yourself,* Gay Hendricks, PhD, (2016) outlined a self-love process. He indicated that the groundwork for self-love is your commitment to accept life for what it is *and* yourself for what you think, feel, desire, and how you've behaved. This acceptance combined with the willingness to love yourself brings you to the experience, in this moment, of loving yourself.

The following is my adaptation of Hendricks's process, modified and elongated to make the transition to self-acceptance and self-love in smaller steps.

Instead of numbing yourself to your current internal state, look inside and:
1. *Become aware* of a current unloving thought, feeling, desire, or behavior.
    a. Thought: *I'm unworthy. No one loves me.*
    b. Feeling: Angry, sad, scared, depressed.
    c. Desire: I want to give up.
    d. Behavior: Sitting home alone all day.

Instead of avoiding the thought, feeling, desire, or behavior through blame of others, excuses, or mood-altering:
2. *Remove resistance* to the unloving thought, feeling, desire, or behavior. Allow your thought, feeling, desire, or behavior to have a place in your life. (It is already present; don't fight its existence.) Rather than keeping this thought, feeling, desire, or

behavior at arm's length, get into it:
3. *Experience reality through acceptance* of the unloving thought, feeling, desire, or behavior.

    a. Accept and experience what you think, feel, or desire, or your behavior as your current response to life.

    b. Also, know these are only your thoughts, feelings, desires, and behavior. They are *not* who you really are.

As you realize your thought, feeling, desire, or behavior is your experience but not you, you can:

4. *Embrace yourself through self-love* by loving yourself while you have the unloving thought, feeling, desire, or behavior.

    a. Say to yourself, "I love myself," while:

        i. Thinking: *I'm unworthy. No one loves me.*

        ii. Feeling: Angry, sad, scared, depressed.

        iii. Desiring: I want to give up.

iv. Behaving: Isolating myself at home.
 b. Find the positive motive under it all. Here: "I value feeling worthy and being worthy."

The key is unconditional acceptance and love for who you are in the moment. Loving yourself while you have these shaming thoughts, uncomfortable or unhappy feelings, or inappropriate desires, or behavior is *loving yourself as you are for who you are.* This experience of self-love will connect you with your essential self.

Hendricks said it helps to remain in this process as long as you can. You'll notice a positive physical and emotional response as you love and celebrate yourself. While it's difficult to always consciously love yourself, make your willingness to do so be a trigger to enter into this process whenever you can.

Here's an example of this process applied to feeling guilty about divorce:
1. *Become aware.* I feel guilty about my actions in my love relationship.

2. *Remove resistance.* I allow that I have guilt about things I did and said in my love relationship. These behaviors occurred, and my feelings of guilt exist.
3. *Experience reality through acceptance.* Though I don't like them, I accept my feelings of guilt as my emotional response to these actions. I realize these feelings are just that, feelings. They are not who I truly am.
4. *Embrace yourself through self-love.* My guilt is an emotional response to my behavior; it's not me. *I love myself while having these feelings of guilt.* This guilt shows that I want to behave differently in the future.

Unlike relationships with others where behavior is the only avenue of connection, the relationship you have with yourself is also expressed in your thoughts, feelings, and desires. Go through the self-love process for an unloving thought, feeling, desire, or behavior. Repeat for any additional ones you want to work on.

1. *Become aware.* (State an unloving thought, feeling, desire, or behavior.)

   _____

   _____

2. *Remove resistance.* (Allow the existence of it in the context of a particular situation.)

   _____

   _____

3. *Experience reality through acceptance.* (State your acceptance of it as your response to this life situation. Also, state your awareness that it is not who you truly are.)

   _____

   _____

4. *Embrace yourself through self-love.* (State your love for yourself while having this thought, feeling, desire, or behavior.) State your healthy intention under it.

   _____

   _____

Self-love affects everything. It connects you within as well as without.

The Being-ness of Self-Love

John Powell (1995) outlined three ingredients in the process of loving in his classic book *Unconditional Love.* He discussed them concerning love with others. Here, I apply them to self-love.

Kindness

Kindness toward self is shown by how well one separates identity from behavior, in other words self-acceptance in the face of mistakes. Muttered words speak volumes: "I'll try again and give it my best effort; I'm okay whatever happens" is an entirely different message than "My God, what's wrong with me?" or "This just proves how stupid I am!" As someone once said, "If your thoughts were food, how healthy would you be eating?"

Kindness is also rooted in an unshakable belief that you are worthy of happiness and a commitment to pursue what that means to you. The outcome is less important than honoring yourself. These help you consider your actions without self-condemnation, an important element of living from the essential self.

Encouragement

Active self-encouragement is unconditional acceptance that sees setbacks as learning opportunities, not failure. Self-love allows us to celebrate who we are and what we do even though it's not perfect. Encouragement is also the belief that we can meet our needs or find resources to help get them met.

Challenge

Challenge is bringing out your self-love to interact with others. In doing so, you help create an atmosphere of love greater than before. Examples:
- Making amends.
- Assertively standing your ground.
- Overcoming a fear or addiction.
- Facing the reality of divorce.
- Offering an opinion.

Perhaps the greatest challenge is to find aspects of yourself that have not been loved. This allows you to increase self-acceptance and self-love.

Assess your kindness, encouragement, and challenge.

Kindness

How well do you value yourself?

1. What is your candid opinion of yourself?
   _____
   _____

   a. What do you say to yourself when you succeed?
   _____
   _____

   b. What do you say to yourself when you fall short?
   _____
   _____

   c. How well do you determine your deepest wants and needs?
   _____
   _____

2. To what extent does your behavior honor these desires with actions?
   _____
   _____

Encouragement

1. How do you encourage yourself to do something new? _____
_____

2. What changes in your life have you generated? _____
_____

3. How do you respond to change? _____
_____

Challenge
What do you believe is your potential in your:
1. Relationship with self: _____
_____

   How close are you to reaching it? _____
   What might you do to achieve it? _____

2. Career: _____
_____

   How close are you to reaching it? _____

What might you do to achieve it? _____

3. Friendships: _____

How close are you to reaching it? _____
What might you do to achieve it? _____

4. Love relationships: _____
How close are you to reaching it? _____
What might you do to achieve it? _____

5. Family and parenting: _____

How close are you to reaching it? _____
What might you do to achieve it? _____

6. Spiritual life: _____

How close are you to reaching it? _____

What might you do to achieve it? _____

Which areas are at or close to your desired state? _____

Which areas need the most improvement? _____

Your reaction: _____

Self-Love and Relationship Loss

Divorce impacts self-love in several ways: doubt concerning life choices, attractiveness and desirability, and confusion about love in yourself and in the universe. It's difficult to be kind while berating yourself over what you did or didn't do. The most self-loving actions are working through feelings of grief, anger, guilt, and shame to clear aside the debris of divorce and reconnect with your essential self.

Loving connections with yourself make it easier to reestablish self-trust. These boost your desirability as a person and your ability to relate. More on this in the chapters on friendships, dating, sexuality, and love relationships.

For now, do the following exercises to uncover self-love during this time of loss.

1. Make a list of eight things you love and admire about yourself. They can be simple, such as "my cooking," "my sense of humor." (Do as many as you can. Expand this list as you build more self-love.)

   I love myself for: _____
   _____
   _____
   _____
   _____
   _____

   a. Spend one minute on each item by reading it aloud and dwelling on the quality or skill.

b. Share this list with a friend, taking in that person's approval, and writing down any additions your friend suggests.

   c. If qualities about yourself that you don't love or admire come to mind, use them to enhance self-love in the next step.

2. Make a list of three thoughts, feelings, desires, or behaviors about yourself that you don't admire or love. *Remember, they are not who you really are!* For each item:

   a. Describe what you intend, for example if you wrote "disorganized," realize that you intend to be organized. Celebrate your positive intention by recognizing it.

   b. Brainstorm three ways you can realize your positive intention.

   c. Examine your "I love myself for" list to see what attributes you already have to assist you.

   d. Identify a resource (person or book for example) that can help you.

   e. Create a plan for change.

    f. For those items you don't desire to change, accept and love yourself by going through the self-love process outlined earlier in this chapter.

1. I don't love myself because I (think, feel, want, act):

   _____

   Positive Intention: _____
   Brainstorm ways to fulfill positive intention:

   _____
   _____

   My positive attributes that can help: _____

   _____

   Resources: _____
   Plan for change: _____

   _____
   _____

2. I don't love myself because I (think, feel, want, act): _____

   Positive Intention: _____

Brainstorm ways to fulfill positive intention: _____

_____

_____

My positive attributes that can help: _____

_____

Resources: _____
Plan for change: _____

_____

_____

3. I don't love myself because I (think, feel, want, act): _____

_____

Positive Intention:
Brainstorm ways to fulfill positive intention: _____

_____

_____

_____

My positive attributes that can help: _____

_____

Resources: _____
Plan for change: _____
_____
_____

Your reactions? How do these exercises bring you closer to self-love?
_____
_____
_____

The Committed Behavior of Self-Love

In all relationships, love is more than an emotional response. Deeds bring love to life. Self-love is demonstrated through the physical, emotional, and intellectual care you give yourself. You cannot love yourself and do harmful things to your body. Here are suggestions with space to describe your current behavior.

Physical
1. Diet: nutritious meals, snacks, and beverages.
   Your diet? _____

2. Exercise: fitness maintained on several levels:
    a. Aerobic: minimum of thirty minutes, five times per week in target range for heart rate according to your age.
    b. Anaerobic: weight training, muscle toning, or stretching.
3. Sleep: adequate nightly amount and daily times of relaxation.
   Your sleep? _____

4. Recreation: stress-reducing and entertaining physical activity.
   Your recreation? _____

Be mindful:
1. Always check with a physician before you begin an exercise program.
2. Recognize that attempts to numb emotional pain through physical activity (compulsive exercise, thrill-seeking, and so forth) likely stem from a hidden desire to release shame-based pain. Channel that desire into caring, not harming, yourself.

Emotional: (What is your current relationship to your feelings?)

1. Awareness of feelings (which ones): _____

2. Appropriate expression of emotions (which ones): _____

3. Awareness of the needs your feelings indicate. List the emotion and corresponding need.

Emotion	Need
(Example: Loneliness)	Connecting with others)

4. Being around supportive people where you can express emotions and get help meeting needs.

5. Emotional care through meditation, prayer, or simply allowing your essential self to communicate with you.
_____
_____

Intellectual
1. Intellectual stimulation through reading, conversation, further education.
Your intellectual stimulation? _____
_____

2. Current pursuits that challenge your skills:
_____

3. Time to dream, fantasize: _____
_____

4. Brainstorming solutions, executing plans: _____
_____

5. Positive thoughts (such as affirmations or self-help reading): _____
_____

6. Other: _____

Validate your self-love as you care for yourself:
- Congratulate yourself for meditating.
- Enjoy nature during your walk; consciously connect your loving self with creation.
- Eat the nutritious snack and feel how you love yourself.

These behaviors not only reinforce your love of self, they help keep you on track with loving thoughts and behaviors. As you do these, unloving thoughts and actions that obscure your destiny of happiness will fall away.

Listen to the Unconditional Self-Love visualization (available at http://www.newharbinger.com/45397). Believe the voice of your essential self.

Nina Remembers... *During a weekend workshop in London, Marian shared that after her brutal divorce experience, she put up her favorite Oscar Wilde quote, "To love oneself is the beginning of a life-long romance." After reading this day after day, she realized she'd begun to believe it.*

Journaling to Freedom

Write a letter to yourself, expressing deep, abiding love. If this is difficult, write a letter loving yourself while having doubts. As your self-love grows, write more letters celebrating it.

Dear Me,

_____
_____
_____
_____
_____
_____
_____
_____

The inner connections of self-love are mirrored by loving connections with friends as you reawaken to life. This is explored in the next chapter.

Action Steps for Moving Onward

As always, share with trusted others.

1. Do the self-love process. Dwell on how this helps you with self-acceptance and self-love.

2. Assess your kindness, encouragement, and challenge. Discuss specific ways you can improve your life and love yourself.

3. Do the assessments on what you love yourself for, what you don't love yourself for, and the changes you can make to fulfill your positive intentions. Take time to journal how this work helps you view yourself more lovingly.

4. Examine your committed behavior of self-love. Choose specific ways you can behave lovingly toward yourself physically, emotionally, and intellectually. Make commitments to a friend to do so and discuss the results. Use these to celebrate yourself.

5. Listen to the Unconditional Self-Love visualization (downloadable audio) at least three times this week and once per week thereafter; journal how this feels.

6. Listen to the Finding My Love meditation (downloadable audio).

7. Write your letter of self-love.

8. For the next week, make a list of what you accomplished each day, even simple actions, such as made my bed or washed the car. Take a few minutes and dwell upon these. Feel acceptance for yourself.

9. Whenever you're not accepting yourself, stop and write ten times: "I love myself while (whatever it is that you do not like)." Stay with this long enough to feel a sense of love for who you are in the present.

Part V

Reawakening to Life

As you heal from your divorce and create a better relationship with yourself, the desire and willingness to relate with others change. The next three chapters look at branching out into social connection and increasing intimacy in all your relationships.

Chapter 15 looks at your history as a friend and discusses how to find friends after divorce to get the support you need.

Chapter 16 goes beyond friendship into sharing physical intimacy and building trust to help you relate in the world.

Chapter 17 explores love and intimacy with self, with dating partners, and in a long-term love-relationship.

Chapter 15

Building Friendships

Friend: *One who knows all about you and loves you just the same.*
—Elbert Hubbard

STEPS ALONG THE WAY

1. **Learning from Your Friendship History**
2. **Building Friendships After Divorce**
3. **Getting Support from Friends**

Friendship is the foundation for any positive personal relationship. This is especially true after divorce. Dr. Bruce Fisher used to describe an "emotional seedbed" analogy about the importance of friendships: for a garden, one prepares the ground before planting; in the same way, you become a healthier love partner when you develop yourself in supportive friendships prior to romantic involvement. This is so because nourishing friendships help you practice relationship skills—commitment, communication, conflict resolution, intimate sharing—without the complications of sexual and romantic involvement.

Let's look at how you've been a friend, ways to reconnect with established friends, and how to find new ones. Then, we'll discuss the best way to get needs met with friends.

Learning from Your Friendship History

Review the psychological needs discussed in chapter 5. Now, list the major friends you've had or currently have. Recall why you became friends and if applicable, why the friendship ended.

Friend	Reason Connected	Reason Ended

Friendship means: _____

The needs I sought to have met by friends: _____

The needs I sought but were not satisfied by friends: _____

Friends' needs I sought to satisfy: _____

What has worked for me in my friendships: _____

What hasn't worked for me in my friendships: _____

Did you have friends of both genders? Why or why not? _____

How well did you replace friends who left? _____

Be aware of patterns. If you've always been a "taker" or a "giver," this knowledge can help you understand why your friendships (and love relationships) were not as balanced as you may have wanted. Watch for trends: lack of friends, similar needs not met by any friends, lack of opposite-sex or same-sex friendships, loss of friends without replacement due to moving, divorce, or other changes.

What patterns do you see? _____

Your reactions: _____

Will's Take *After my divorce, I realized I hadn't ever been friends with women. They'd been either dating partners or acquaintances. It's been rewarding to create friendships with females. I've also become a better friend to males by being involved in a men's group. These friendships have deepened my quality of life and enhanced all my relationships, including the one with myself.*

Building Friendships After Divorce

Connecting with Established Friends

During divorce, some individuals pull away from friends out of fear of rejection. Since many friends are part of a couple, difficulties may occur:

- Some couple friends may feel awkward relating to you as a single person.
- One partner may fear you'll become a rival in their relationship.
- They have their own loss issues about your divorce.
- They don't want to take sides.

- A fear that divorce may be "catching."

If your divorce loss is compounded by abandonment from couple-friends, realize that this says more about them than about you. Don't let fear of this be a barrier. What may seem like lack of support may simply be an oversight as they deal with issues in their own lives.

Communicate before you make any lasting decisions about established friends. Be clear with your needs and requests, for example, "I'm feeling lonely right now and would like to share some time with you," "I need to express my grief (or anger or other emotion). Do you have time to listen?" Most likely, a willing friend will respond. If the other person is vague or not forthcoming, you can decide whether the friendship is worth risking a discussion. Of course, finding new friends who are also working through divorce can be rewarding and supportive. The key is to know your friendship needs and reach out to those who demonstrate a willingness to connect.

Finding New Friends

Divorce is traumatic. It's as if your skin is sunburned, painful to touch. Yet, you need touch to feel accepted. Platonic friendships can meet needs for emotional intimacy and physical connection without the vulnerabilities of romance. With friends, you can share thoughts, feelings, wants and needs, and nonsexual touch (such as hugs). Friendships also help you begin a new social life by safely exploring activities as a newly single person.

Examine your current attitudes about friendships. Confine your answers to specific behaviors, for example punctual, good listener. Avoid feelings and desires, such as valued, nurtured. This is important because relationships with others consist of behavior not the thoughts, feelings, and desires of either partner.

1. What do you look for in a same-sex friend? _____

2. What do you look for in an opposite-sex friend? _____

3. What are friendship activities? _____

4. What are the limits of friendship, such as affection, financial, time? _____

   Your reactions: _____

Who?
You can best determine who is compatible when you know these characteristics about yourself:
- Your talents and abilities so you can find people who are similar to you.
- Your interests so you can find those who engage in activities you wish to learn.

Personal Talents and Abilities Inventory
   Make a list of your talents and abilities, for example fishing, hiking, playing the guitar, involvement in church, sharing thoughts and feelings. Add more as you can. Don't fall into the low self-image trap of "I'm not good

at anything." Make this list when you feel positive about yourself.

1. _____
2. _____
3. _____
4. _____
5. _____
6. _____

Interests Inventory

List five interests, what you would like to learn or improve, such as playing the piano, dancing, carpentry. Add more as you think of them.

1. _____
2. _____
3. _____
4. _____
5. _____

Now, combine this information with the Relating Desires Assessment in chapter 5 and you have a profile not only of yourself but also of the traits and interests of people with whom you could readily build friendships. By getting involved in activities that correspond to your talents and abilities, you'll automatically meet others like you. When you actively engage in activities you want to learn, you'll connect with those who can teach you and build commonalities.

Where?

Social environments can be divided into two categories (Limón and Whalen 1986): temporary settings and continuing settings.

Temporary settings are limited in duration, usually involve large amounts of people, and typically promote brief encounters. Attending communicates common interest. Examples:
- Conferences
- Auditoriums
- Friends' weddings
- Airports
- Museums
- Shopping
- Zoo
- Sports activities
- Dog parks
- Parties
- Walking
- Dances
- While traveling
- Sporting events

Positive elements of temporary settings are the ease with which you may move around and the relative anonymity of attendance. A negative characteristic is that the reason for attendance is somewhat general. This makes connecting dependent on introducing yourself and making small talk.

Continuing settings are more specific, are often concerning an interest or activity, and foster repeat interactions. Examples:
- Theater club
- Investment club
- Volunteering
- Business groups
- Social clubs
- Travel tours
- Colleges
- Political committees
- Block party
- Brewpubs
- Flag football
- Religious organizations
- Dance schools
- Classes
- Conservation group
- Choir

- Employment

The advantages of a continuing setting are commonality of interest and the likelihood that repeated meetings will increase interaction.

Some settings are both temporary and continuing due to the length and habit of attendance. For example, a one-time lecture at the university is temporary. Taking a class makes it a continuing setting. Examples:
- Religious organization
- Library
- Fitness centers
- Resorts
- Colleges
- Brewpubs
- Work
- Bookstores

Fill out the Meeting Friends Blueprint below. For each talent and ability you listed before, brainstorm a specific temporary or continuing setting or both in your area where others with similar talents and abilities would be. Get suggestions from others.

Talent or Ability	Temporary Setting	Continuing Setting
(Example: Play violin)	Concerts	Community orchestra)

For three interests, brainstorm a specific temporary or continuing setting both in your area where others with similar interests and abilities would be.

Interest	Temporary Setting	Continuing Setting
(Example: Gourmet cooking)	Food convention	Cooking class)

Your life is in your hands. When you start to reach out, others will respond, but *you must take the first steps.*

Nina Remembers... *A woman in an Australian seminar shared that she'd always had both male and female friends. Then, after a whirlwind courtship, her new husband demanded that she have only women friends. To save her* *marriage, she agreed. Recognizing the harm in this, she made the most loving choice for herself and ended the relationship. Smiling, with tearful eyes, she told how whole and free she felt to have male friends again.*

The Role of Social Media

Social media is a proven medium for people to connect on multiple platforms. With an ever-changing landscape, it would be foolhardy to attempt any discussion of specific apps or web sites. However, we can look at the benefits of social media as well as the drawbacks.

Benefits

Smartphones have allowed us to communicate with almost everyone, everywhere, making connections with family and established friends much easier. One can find old friends, classmates, and distant relatives with ease. Internet platforms provide a place to share thoughts, feelings, activities, photos, and videos. They've made it possible to be "present" together even when we're in different locales.

Obtaining information about clubs, interest groups, and events facilitates the search to find new friends. Dating sites have multiple ways to find, learn about, and contact seemingly compatible dating partners who can become "just" friends if romantic considerations change. (We'll have more discussion on this in the next two chapters.)

Drawbacks

Besides the obvious frustrations of being available to nearly everyone, including being "followed" by one's ex-partner, the drawbacks of social media are rooted in your values. What do you want in a friend? This is especially important after relationship loss when loneliness and grief are present. Electronic connections, be they text, instant message, or email can provide caring thoughts and encouragements, but they cannot give you tone of voice or the human contact necessary for us as human beings. Even video calls that do allow for aural and visual connection eventually lead to the loneliness of longing for a simple hug. Any relationship is limited if in-person contact doesn't occur. The warmth of human touch and the vulnerabilities of fully connecting are what create the intimacy we desire in our friendships.

Ultimately, use social media as a tool to find, create, and enhance your friendships. Don't let its platforms become a substitute for in-person relating. Online relationships can limit the risk of vulnerabilities, but that prevents meaningful sharing and sabotages the deepest of human desires: to be known and loved as ourselves.

How?

How to approach someone depends on the setting and the activity. It's different in a bar than in a pottery class. This underscores the advantages of a continuing setting in which common activity serves as an icebreaker.

For temporary settings, other tactics are necessary. Make conscious contact with another person by:
- Asking friendly questions
- Sharing about yourself

- Learning to make small talk (weather, sports, noncontroversial topics)
- Becoming someone who others can approach, for example make eye contact and smile.

Not always, but many times your interest will be reciprocated. This will create opportunities to develop acquaintances that may become friends. Possibly, some may evolve into dating relationships.

Listen to the Healthy Friendships visualization (available at http://www.newharbinger.com/45397) to encourage you in your efforts.

Getting Support from Friends

Divorce recovery brings many concerns: financial security, raising children, housing issues, coping with career, as well as qualms about another love relationship. Friends can provide emotional support and suggest ideas to cope. You can best receive their support when you focus your interactions. These three steps will help you.

1. Determine Your Needs

Write down your three biggest fears.

1. _____
2. _____
3. _____

Pick one and outline your thoughts, feelings, needs, and abilities to deal with it. Also, list your values (how life should be lived) concerning it. Use this process to help you with any issue or emotion. Brainstorming your current abilities keeps you aware of your values.

Example:

Fear: Repeating Past Relationship Mistakes

Thoughts: *I think I don't make good relationship choices.*

Feelings: Fear, anger, frustration, depression, anxiety.

Needs: I don't want to be in another painful love relationship. I need to learn how to have good relationships.

Abilities: I can make friends with others who face divorce. I can find out why I divorced and learn what to do to create better relationships.

Values: I believe that healthy love relationships are nurturing to both partners. I deserve a good relationship.

Your fear: _____
Thoughts: _____

Feelings: _____

Needs: _____

Abilities: _____

Values: _____

Your reactions: _____

2. Identify and Communicate with Chosen Friends

Choose those family members and friends who listen in an accepting, nonshaming way. Avoid those who give prescriptive answers like, "All you have to do is _____, and everything will be fine." Also, stay away from others who

judge you or try to find you another love-partner to take your pain away. Spend time with those who truly support you when they:
- Listen to your needs and give their opinions when asked
- Allow you to feel the pain and confusion while offering shoulders to cry on
- Encourage as you scream out your anger
- Give nonsexual hugs
- Provide you with nourishing meals and child care when you need space.

Now, choose a list of at least six support people, of both sexes if possible, with whom you can share your needs and feelings. Write each name and their relationship to you (sister, friend, coworker). If you are not able to think of six people, this shows you need to build more supportive friendships. Joining a divorce-recovery seminar can be a highly effective way to create an almost "instant" support group. Of course, this only works when you're willing to become actively involved.

Name	Relationship to You

Next, decide when, where, and what you will share with your support person. This always involves risk. (Holding thoughts, feelings, and needs inside is also risky.) Decide what you want to discuss, then determine who you want share with. Make an appointment. This sets the stage for getting support.

Example:
> **Fear:** Repeating Past Relationship Mistakes
> **Who:** my good friend Randy.
> **When:** noon on Friday.
> **Where:** Pablo's Mexican Restaurant.

Make an appointment for the previous fear you identified. (Do more if you can.) Follow through by attending, sharing, and receiving support.

> **Fear:** _____

Who: _____
When: _____
Where: _____

Remember, an appointment is for you to get support and brainstorm solutions. Sometimes, all that's needed is connection and recreation. However, distracting from feelings or needs rather than talking about them only bottles up the pain and creates more stress. Do the necessary work first. After that, activities will be more fun.

3. Careful Consideration of Suggestions

Others' support may be totally inappropriate. For example, you share with a friend your fear of not being attractive. That person attempts to dispel your fear by suggesting that you have sex together. This "suggestion" makes it obvious that this individual is not the friend you thought you had.

More likely, friends and family will give well-meaning advice. Some of it may be meant to placate you; some may bring up more fears; other suggestions may have elements that can help. Consider suggestions by comparing them to your values, regarding your feelings (but do not be controlled by them), and determining what assists your healing and growth. Use this framework to guide you:

1. *Research ideas* using your support system and brainstorm ways to meet the needs or cope with the issues you have.
2. *Evaluate components.* Ask yourself:
   a. Do these suggestions address my need?
   b. What are the benefits?
   c. What are the obstacles?
   d. Do these fit my values?
3. *Listen to feelings,* especially those beneath your surface emotion.
4. *Consider your healing process.* How does this behavior or activity enhance your self-respect?
5. *Create a plan* that provides a balance of support, prudent risk, and growth.
6. *Work your plan* and evaluate it along the way, paying close attention both to what you think *and* feel.

   Example:

Fear: Dating Again

1. *Research ideas.* You share with a friend your fear of dating and being out in the "singles world." Your friend invites you to go out with a group to a concert. You mention your fear about running into your former love partner. Your friend commits to stay by your side during the evening and assures you that the group will not go anywhere you believe your ex-partner might be.

2. *Evaluate components.*

    a. *Does this address my need?* While not a "date," it can approximate some of the logistics: what to wear, how to act, making conversation, learning to enjoy a night out.

    b. *What are the benefits?* It's probably the easiest way to break the ice after divorce. Supportive others will be close at hand.

    c. *What are the obstacles?* Finding motivation and energy. Overcoming the fear of being where my ex-partner may be.

    d. *Do these ideas fit my values?* Yes. I deserve a happy, healthy social life. I want to enjoy others' company, feel comfortable as a single, and eventually go on an individual date.
3. *Listen to feelings.* I'm scared. Underneath, I have excitement mixed with sadness. Also, I have determination to move on with my life.
4. *Consider your healing process.* This feels like a big stretch, but it will be good for me to stop isolating. Eventually, I must confront the discomfort of a new social life. This is good for my healing process.
5. *Create a plan.* I plan to attend the concert. My friend will drive. Afterward, we'll go to a restaurant where it's highly unlikely my ex-partner would be.
6. *Work your plan.*

   Use this strategy for a fear or need. Remember, your new life is entirely in your hands.

   Fear or need: _____
1. *Research ideas:* _____

2. *Evaluate components:*
   a. Does this address my need? _____
   b. What are the benefits? _____
   c. What are the obstacles? _____
   d. Do these ideas fit my values? _____

3. *Listen to feelings:* _____

4. *Consider your healing process:* _____

5. *Create a plan:* _____

6. *Work your plan* (and evaluate): _____

Your reactions: _____

While nothing will instantly resolve the difficulties of divorce recovery, you can build a support system that'll help you cope when things get tough, one that mirrors your resilience to bounce back. Listen to the Healthy Connections visualization (available at http://www.newharbinger.com/45397) to help you become involved in interactions with helpful friends and family.

Journaling to Freedom

Write a letter to your current and future friends about what you want to have in friendship. Share your intentions to talk with them, cry with them, laugh, and play together. Express your heart's desire to know and be known.

Dear Friends,

As you build friendships in your new life, stirrings of a different nature are bound to occur. These usher in a new and exciting aspect of growth. The next chapter, on exploring sexuality and trust, will delve into these.

Action Steps for Moving Onward

Share with trusted friends or family.

1. Assess your beliefs and history about friends. Determine your needs.

2. Examine your attitudes about friendships after divorce. Discuss with supportive others, especially with

those who have experienced the ending of a love relationship.

3. Do the Personal Talents and Abilities Inventory and the Interests Inventory. Spend time this week expanding these lists.

4. Make out your Meeting Friends Blueprint for both talents or abilities and interests. Try one new setting for a talent, ability, or interest. Be aware of your thoughts and feelings as you do so; take note of how your life changes.

5. Determine your friendship needs, how you can get support from friends, and how you can evaluate that support to meet your needs.

6. Work the support plan for a fear or need. Use careful consideration. Follow through on your plan and evaluate.

7. Listen to the Healthy Friendships and Healthy Connections visualizations (downloadable audio files) at least three times this week.

8. Listen to the Warmth of Friendship meditation (downloadable audio).

9. Write your letter to friends and share with a trusted friend and new friends too. Make this a part of your celebration of life.

Chapter 16

Exploring Sexuality and Trust

As you think, you travel, and as you love, you attract.
—James Allen

STEPS ALONG THE WAY

1. **The Three Stages of Sexuality After Divorce**
2. **Some Potential Pitfalls and Benefits of Exploring Sexuality**
3. **Ways to Communicate Sexual Interest**
4. **Building Trust**

After divorce, being single can be confusing. Those whose love relationships lasted for decades find much different gender expectations and behavior than those who are younger or whose relationships were shorter in length, for example women are independent and assertive; men are caught between intellectual acceptance of women as initiators and emotional discomfort. Sexual freedom is exciting but tempered by one's morality and the risks of sexually transmitted infections. Most find that feeling sexual is one thing; acting on those urges is something else.

Behaviors concerning when, how, and with whom to express sexuality vary. We'll explore the full range of what these might be. No judgment is made about any approach. Take from this chapter what fits your values and morality. However you choose to express sexuality, these explorations can help you understand yourself better.

The Three Stages of Sexuality After Divorce

There are three stages in the sexuality rebuilding block (Fisher and Alberti 2016):
1. Lack of interest from being in deep emotions of loss.
2. Horny stage where strong sexual urges surface.
3. Normal sex drive resumes.

We'll describe all three stages as well as the potential pitfalls and benefits of exploring sexuality. You'll define your sexuality and determine ways to express it. Finally, we'll look at rebuilding trust, an important prerequisite for sharing ourselves in all relationships.

Stage One: Lack of Interest

When submerged in grief and anger, divorcing individuals often lack interest in anything sexual. Still, they desire skin contact to alleviate loneliness, and some try sex as a way to meet this need. In a one-night-stand situation, a man may suddenly be impotent or a woman uncharacteristically nonresponsive, and this can leave one feeling terribly damaged. Realize that emotional pain saps your energy, and you don't have the comfort level to respond sexually as you have in the past. The danger here is that a person may think something is physically wrong. If this has happened to you, know it's a normal reaction to having deep pain from divorce. As you heal, you'll return to your normal level of sexual functioning.

For most people, lack of interest doesn't last. Working through the grief and anger sparks renewed sexual energy.

Stage Two: Horny

In areas of the far north, summer is only a few weeks long. Intense mating occurs as animals reawaken to biological urges. This is also true for those completing the cold winter of relationship loss. Released from unhappy unions where sex may have been perfunctory or nonexistent, many individuals want to explore the singles life to find out what they've been missing. It can be exciting, frustrating, and scary.

Open up to the excitement of sexuality without being overwhelmed by its temptations. You may want to let go and have fun. If it fits with your moral standards, do so, but do it wisely. Careless actions can compound emotional pain and cause physical injury. Sexuality is a joyful challenge. Honor yourself and others with your behavior.

The horny stage usually doesn't last forever. After making choices about expressing your sexuality and relating with others, the newness of exploration wears off, and you'll find more stability in your desires. You'll also feel more secure as yourself. This brings you to the stability stage.

Stage Three: Stability

Here, you're ready to move beyond sex into a fuller experience of sexuality because you have deeper empathy and are more able to relate physically and emotionally. Life opens up like the flower bud relaxing into radiant bloom.

Benefits of the Stability Stage
- You'll have a better relationship with yourself.
- You'll build trust and be better able take risks and deal with rejection and ending of relationships.
- By being more vulnerable, you'll be more intimate.
- You'll gain more knowledge and courage to consider a committed love relationship.

- You'll be open to remaining in dating mode or to choosing a committed love relationship.

Some Potential Pitfalls and Benefits of Exploring Sexuality

Pitfalls
- Drawing long-range conclusions from short-term intensity.
- Believing only what's positive and screening out the negative. (Antidote: stay grounded in reality.)
- Projecting into the future after a few encounters.
- Believing that divorce pain is magically over.
- Seeking physical intimacy as a cure-all. Watch out for:
    - Self-esteem dependent on outcome.
    - Promiscuity can promote sex addiction.
    - Shallow physical intimacy masquerades as real intimacy and tempts, creating unsatisfactory

relationships, which keeps you from creating healthy ones.
* Sexually transmitted infection and disease.
* Becoming dependent on artificial or dangerous stimulation. Relying on alcohol to relax, or pornography, chronic masturbation, or affairs to become turned on detracts from a healthy social life.
* Believing that a good sexual relationship will only happen with one particular person. What's important is the experience of connection. If a greater union evolves, wonderful. Don't think that only one person can meet your needs. This attitude sabotages relationships.

Your reactions: _____

Benefits
* A reawakened sexual self. Others finding you attractive enhances self-image and attractiveness.
* Finding sex drive again.
* Discovering your abilities to appropriately interact, initiate, and

respond builds confidence in your sexual self and as a whole person.
- Learning to be intimate. Physical intimacy sets the stage for deeper intellectual and emotional intimacy with others and yourself, for example "pillow talk."
- Different partners teach valuable lessons. You learn what does and doesn't feel good. This helps you make better choices.
- Putting sex and sexuality into perspective helps you seek a mature relationship that includes sex and a whole lot more.

Your reactions: _____
_____
_____

In our society, sex and intercourse have overshadowed the more encompassing quality of sexuality as part of our humanness. In the Rebuilding divorce-recovery seminars, participants often define sexuality beyond sexual behaviors into the full range of intimacy and spirituality. Define your beliefs so you can choose what's best for you. Return to these to see if your attitudes and values about sex and sexuality change.

Sexuality is: _____
_____

Sex means: _____
_____

Now complete the following sentences; include all aspects of sexual behavior. (Add more as you can.)

Satisfying sexual activity involves:
1. _____
2. _____
3. _____
4. _____
5. _____
6. _____

How do these change your overall definition of sexuality? _____

Examine your attitudes about sexual expression. For each of the following, explore both sides.
1.   Abstinence
      Reasons for: _____
      Reasons against: _____
2.   Masturbation
      Reasons for: _____

Reasons against: _____
3. Nonromantic friendship sex
   Reasons for: _____
   Reasons against: _____
4. Sex in nonmonogamous relationship
   Reasons for: _____
   Reasons against: _____
5. Sex in a monogamous relationship
   Reasons for: _____
   Reasons against: _____
   Your reactions: _____

___

___

Based on your values about sexuality and sexual behavior, which of these behaviors meet your particular goals during this stage of your recovery?

___

___

Ways to Communicate Sexual Interest

Most communication occurs through actions and nonverbal components of speech. Congruence in behavior and words is essential. Also, your behavior must express your values, concerning what you want, how you'll satisfy your wants and needs, and how you'll satisfy your partner's wants and needs.

Communicating accurately about sexual involvement takes place over several stages of interaction. Here are four progressive levels of involvement (Gorski 1993, 236–240).

1. *Desire* is an inner dialog within oneself.
2. *Romantic attention* communicates desire through body language (eye contact, smiling, physical proximity) and other nonverbal cues (voice tone); verbally, this can involve suggestive topics, joking, teasing.
3. *Affectionate touch* includes handholding, arms around waists, hugging, kissing on the cheek, also prolonged eye contact.
4. *Sexual intimacy* ranges from full-mouth or French kissing; petting with clothes on or off; arousal to orgasm manually, orally, or through intercourse.

Each level uses specific behaviors that increase communication and relax boundaries. If you choose, send signals indicating desired behavior. Look for clear signals from others about willingness to reciprocate. Confusion fosters misunderstanding and can create difficulties from simple embarrassment to assault and rape.

Here's a framework that can help you communicate desires about sex:
1. *Conditions:* what prompts you to want greater intimacy.
2. *Boundaries:* physical, emotional, and intellectual limits of your involvement.
3. *Signals:* specific behavior, verbal and nonverbal, that you would use to communicate your desire to relate or limit or end your interaction.

Example for Romantic Attention

Conditions: Talking one-on-one, eye contact, smiling, laughing, maintaining interaction. (You could include physical appearance as well as topics of discussion.)

Boundaries: Discuss noncontroversial topics, avoiding

previous relationships, family history, or deep emotions. No touching unless responding to other's casual touch.

Signals to communicate desire to relate:
a. Verbal: Compliment appearance. Ask questions about interests, connection to this gathering. Share enjoyment of conversation.
b. Nonverbal: Smiling, leaning forward. If appropriate, whisper a joke or observation about the gathering, and so on. Voice tone friendly, soft.

Signals to communicate limiting or ending interaction:
a. Verbal: Decline to discuss topics, thoughts, or emotions. Decline requests for contact information or to leave with that person. Engage someone else in conversation.
b. Nonverbal: Move back, speak formally, less eye contact, stop smiling, turn away.

Accurate communication can help you interact with more confidence. If the other person doesn't engage in the same ways, this shows less interest. If the response is more intense than you desire, this is your cue to lessen interaction. If the other person is unclear, you can choose to talk about this, break off the interaction, or continue on to get better information.

Build your own strategies for each category.
1.   Desire
        a. Conditions: _____

        b. Boundaries: _____

        c. Signals (None at this level of involvement)
2.   Romantic Attention
        a. Conditions: _____

        b. Boundaries: _____

        c. Signals to communicate my desire to relate:
        Verbal: _____

        Nonverbal: _____

d. Signals to communicate limiting or ending interaction:
Verbal: _____

Nonverbal: _____

3. Affectionate Touch
   a. Conditions: _____

   b. Boundaries: _____

   c. Signals to communicate my desire to relate:
   Verbal: _____

   Nonverbal: _____

   d. Signals to communicate limiting or ending interaction:
   Verbal: _____

   Nonverbal: _____

4. Sexual Intimacy

a. Conditions: _____

b. Boundaries: _____

c. Signals to communicate my desire to relate:
Verbal: _____

Nonverbal: _____

d. Signals to communicate limiting or ending interaction:
Verbal: _____

Nonverbal: _____

How do you think and feel about approaching social situations this way? _____

Dealing with Disease

Sexual expression risks exposure to sexually transmitted infections and diseases. *Literally, you can be risking your life if you have unprotected sex with a new partner!* While there are medications for disease, perhaps the best path is protected sex, which has two dimensions: physical protection and partner protection.

Physical Protection

Only abstinence provides complete physical protection from the exchange of bodily fluids (especially semen, blood, or vaginal secretion) that may contain STI or the HIV virus, which has been shown to cause AIDS. These bodily fluids can enter your body through the penis, the vagina, the anus, the mouth, or any cut or open sore. Care must be taken that these fluids are not exchanged either before, during, or after orgasm and intercourse. Having sex when drunk or high may limit your ability to carefully use proper protected-sex procedures.

Consult your public health department or go online to the Centers for Disease Control website for more specific guidelines about protected sex and the latest information about HIV and other sexually transmitted infections and disease. Keep in mind that protected sex is only "safer" sex and is not 100 percent safe.

Partner Protection

A good lover is a safe lover. You can *never* assume that another person is "safe" regardless of age, looks, perceived trustworthiness, or words. People may truly believe they're not infected and still be carrying STDs in dormant stage.

Be willing to communicate your concerns. This is usually awkward, but *very necessary* because you need to determine whether a potential partner is in a high-risk group, is willing to engage in protected sex, and respects you enough to communicate. Then, you can make an informed decision. Consider the following four points:

1. *Know your own policy* concerning safer sex.
2. *Talk well before becoming intimate.* The "heat of the moment" is the wrong time. Discuss the risk of disease as part of getting to know someone. This gives insight into that person's self-care and helps you find out

if he or she is in a high-risk group for disease: intravenous drug use, anal intercourse, multiple sex partners, unprotected sex practices.
3. *Be honest in your discussions.* Don't hint around; diseases won't. Here are two ways you can broach the subject:

• "This feels embarrassing, but I think it's important to talk about safer sex."

• "I care about me and you. Let's talk about sexual protection."

The other person may well be relieved and respond. If not, then you must decide whether you're willing to risk your health.

4. *Make safer sex fun.* Get different condoms and experiment.

Bottom line, *don't have sex* (Gorski 1993, 235):

• To make the other person change or alter their relationship with you
• From obligation
• From guilt
• If safety is not present.

A Matter of Consent

The alarmingly high rate of sexual assault in society speaks in part to the lack of communication between potential partners. Communication is more than using the same words. It's "shared meaning." Just as you need to be clear about what you want and don't want in a sexual encounter, you need to clearly understand what your partner wants and doesn't want. Ask to be sure there is consent. If not sure, stop until it's clear. And this applies not just to "having sex" but to each activity. Also, be aware that desires change. Alter your behavior when that happens, both to underscore your changed desires and to respond to any changes in your partner.

Intimacy is often different for different people. With clear consent, something exciting and wonderful can happen. Without it, fear, uncertainty, and mistrust can needlessly derail a potentially positive connection or put you in a dangerous situation, physically and legally. And remember: *No means no. Stop means stop.* Both partners have the right to change their minds, set new boundaries, and end an encounter without receiving putdowns, threats, or emotional or physical injury.

Use the Sexual Exploration visualization (available at http://www.newharbinger.com/45397) to help you have healthy experiences during this part of your journey up the rebuilding blocks.

Building Trust

Trust is a big issue, especially after divorce. It's natural to be mistrustful of others because one's love wound is so raw. This attitude helps you avoid another love relationship before you're ready. At the same time, newly divorced people are often untrustworthy themselves. They want to protect against the pain of another loss and may not even trust their own choices. Examples:
- Failing to show up for a date.
- Going on a date but calling a friend and saying, "Come get me. I can't handle this. It's too scary."
- Promising to dance then avoiding the other person.

Until your love wound heals, understand that you're going to be both mistrustful and untrustworthy.

Since we tend to relate with others who are at the same level as us, trustworthiness must begin inside ourselves. The issue is not "Who can I find that's trustworthy?" but "How trustworthy am I?" Finding trust in you fosters the strength and courage to share intimately.

The growth of trust begins slowly. At first, you may desire honest connection but don't feel comfortable or able to pursue one. As you gain a deeper sense of self through your recovery work with grief, anger, fear, and loneliness, you'll have a greater capacity to relate with others. Yet, since healing has not been completed, you have what psychologists call an "approach-nonapproach" style of intimacy. "Come close and be with me, but don't come too close. Keep your distance, but don't go too far away either." It can create a confusing, emotional push-pull that causes "emotional whiplash" in your dating relationships.

Trust appears in your life when you have healed enough to believe in yourself, when your actions match your words, and you know *you* can be trusted:
- "I'll get those tickets and pick you up at 6:00p.m. I'll be there."
- "We'll do this on the weekend. I wouldn't miss it."
- "I'll commit to this relationship."

Rebuild trust slowly as you heal your feelings, raise self-image and self-worth, establish healthy friendships, and learn to be comfortable venturing out as a single person. *When you know you can be trusted, an amazing thing happens. You realize that others can also be trusted.* They go together.

Changing yourself transforms your world. Building trust and exploring your sexuality make way for even greater changes both within yourself and with those around you. We'll look at these in the next chapter, on singleness, relatedness, and love.

Journaling to Freedom

Write a letter to you and proclaim your confidence to maintain healthy boundaries while sharing yourself with others. State your desires and willingness to date and express your sexuality within your values.

Dear Me,

_____
_____
_____
_____
_____
_____
_____
_____

Action Steps for Moving Onward

As always, discuss the results of your assessments with a trusted friend or support group.

1. Give your reactions to the pitfalls and benefits of exploring sexuality.

2. Clarify your values and behaviors around sexuality.

3. Work out your strategies for interacting about sexuality. Consider

how these fit with your morals and values.

4. Listen to the Sexual Exploration visualization (downloadable audio) at least three times this week.

5. Listen to the Scars on My Heart meditation (downloadable audio).

6. Write your letter on expressing your sexuality in a healthful manner.

7. Have fun on a social outing, in a group, or one-on-one.

Chapter 17

Sharing Intimacy: Singleness, Relatedness, and Love

No man is an island.
—John Donne

STEPS ALONG THE WAY

1. **What Is Intimacy?**
2. **Exploring Singleness**
3. **Relatedness — Growing Relationships That Heal**
4. **Choosing Love**

After divorce, being intimate again may seem scary. But it can be a joyous experience when you communicate your needs and get them met while satisfying those of another. We'll look at intimacy with self in singleness and with others through relatedness with others in what Fisher and Alberti (2017) call "growing relationships." Then, we'll explore intimacy in a loving, committed relationship.

What Is Intimacy?

The word "intimacy" comes from the early Latin word "intimus," meaning "inmost." You can think of inti-macy as "into-me-see." One way to define it is "the willingness to risk being vulnerable" (Masters, Johnson, and Kolodny 1988, 252). This means intimacy occurs when each partner shares vulnerabilities—those thoughts, feelings, desires, and actions that are sensitive for each individual. Exchanged, these vulnerabilities allow each partner to "see" into the other. Your vulnerabilities may not be the same as those of others; for example sharing emotions may be difficult for you and easy for your partner. Conversely, sharing ideas and fantasies may be simple for you and a struggle for your partner. For these exchanges to deepen your relationship, both partners must respect each other's vulnerable areas.

The types of intimacy are physical (sharing one's body), intellectual (sharing thoughts, fantasies, and judgments), and emotional (sharing feelings) (Limón and Whalen 1986). Taken together, these add up to sharing one's total self, which then becomes a fourth type: spiritual (sharing humanness). While many people perceive physical sex as intense intimacy, for most it's more vulnerable, and more intimate, to share emotions because it reveals that which is most personal.

Here's an important key: intimacy is the result of *behavior* between two people (Limón and Whalen 1986). It doesn't come from what is thought, felt, or desired. To have an intimate relationship (exchange of vulnerabilities), you cannot simply *act* intimately (sharing vulnerabilities through physical, thoughts, feelings, desires, and actions). You must *behave in ways that foster intimate behavior from your partner* (exchange). When you feel intimate, it's because you believe your real self is accepted and feel safe enough to be who you really are. The same is true for your partner. When these occur together, beautiful things happen.

Consider your former love relationship. In the beginning, intimacy increased as accepting behavior built trust, safety, and the desire to be close. No doubt your relationship ended somewhere on a continuum of diminished intimacy: the slow deterioration of trust through covert or subtle distancing behavior on one end or that sudden rejection and betrayal that come from an extramarital affair on the other.

Recall the discussion on how love is learned in chapter 14. Just as one's family of origin teaches love, it's also the first school of intimacy where the behavior and attitudes of vulnerability exchange are learned (Limón and Whalen 1986, 133). When hugs and kisses are given, the child experiences intimate behaviors of caring, affection, and love. When thoughts and feelings are honored, the child learns how to express self and how to respect the vulnerabilities of self and others. If these are incomplete or missing, the child doesn't learn healthy intimacy. This affects all adult relationships.

Divorced people often blame the lack of intimate connections on their former love partner. Yet, divorce is a tremendous catalyst for recognizing deficiencies in one's own intimacy skills, taking responsibility for them, and motivating change. (Apply the categories of the Comparison: Desired vs. Actual Intimacy in chapter 2 to yourself.) Instead of blaming, understand your part and learn what to do differently. Then, you'll be better able to relate with others who offer nourishing intimacy.

Directions for Growth After Divorce

Many people in shame-based families grew up equating intimacy and love with pain because parenting figures expressed "love" through put-downs, neglect, or physical abuse (Gorski 1993). This upbringing promotes two extremes:
- Some people keep love partners at arm's length to avoid being hurt again.
- Others seek shaming partners to perpetuate pain in a misguided

attempt to feel "love" the only way they know.

Healing both after divorce is essential. We've been working on much of this all along and will do more in this chapter. Here's a brief summary of the steps to healing:

1. Release shame and develop your five freedoms.
2. Uncover self-love and improve self-image and self-esteem.
3. Become assertive and build healthy boundaries—so that involvement need not mean being invaded, and so there's no need to distance oneself for protection.
4. Create healthy friendships.
5. Branch out slowly into mutually respectful dating relationships.

A good relationship has healthy, balanced partners—two people willing *and* able to do what it takes to make it so. Now is the perfect time for you to concentrate on your half of the equation. Since healthy intimacy begins with you, let's look at singleness, the rebuilding block that celebrates your individuality. We've done a ton of work already on building self-image and self-worth. Let's take it further.

Exploring Singleness

During divorce recovery, your choice to spend time with another coexists with spending time developing yourself, what Fisher and Alberti call "singleness." Singleness fosters maturity and independence that's a foundation for a healthy self. It also helps you maintain that self within the boundaries of a friendship, dating, or committed relationship.

Will's Take *In chapter 5, on overcoming loneliness, I shared solo activities: playing my French horn up in the mountains and going to a movie. These were behaviors of singleness.*

Pitfalls and Benefits of Singleness

The benefits of singleness far outweigh the pitfalls. However, both have issues to keep in mind.

Pitfalls
- Economic effects. Two people can make a bigger income than one.

- Unfortunately, women still suffer from wage discrimination.
- While choosing to remain single is an acceptable alternative in today's society, some people may view a single person as only "half" of a whole. Also, some individuals still see "coupleship" as the most desired state.
- One may hide in singleness to avoid vulnerabilities. Fear of relationship loss, rejection, and intimacy, and replaying old habits and relationships can make singleness a safe haven, preventing a person from seeking desired connection.

Benefits
- Reawaken to inner self: thoughts, feelings, desires.
- Sense of security, peace.
- Learn to express yourself: new activities.
- Provide for yourself.
- Don't need another to feel good about yourself.
- Can choose to be alone or with others.

- Don't have to adjust to another's habits.
- Take the time to heal.

Brainstorm activities you enjoy by yourself. Use these as a starting place to develop your individuality. If you choose, share these activities to build friendships. Most importantly, these activities express your ability to enjoy yourself alone. List activities you already enjoy by yourself. Inventory other activities you aren't doing, either ones you already know or would like to learn. For each, rate on a scale of 1 (low) to 10 (high) your level of interest. Add more as you can. (These build on the solo activities you listed in chapters 5 and 6.)

Current list	Rating
1.	
2.	
3.	
4.	
5.	
6.	

Desired list	Rating
1.	
2.	
3.	
4.	
5.	
6.	

Pick two from each list and make specific plans to experience them.

Current activity	Where	When
1.		
2.		
Desired activity	Where	When
1.		
2.		

How does it feel to plan your singleness activities? _____

***Nina Remembers...** A woman in London shared her devastation when her husband left her for a woman the same age as their daughter. This deep pain became the catalyst for her growth. She worked through Rebuilding and found she could accept, trust, and love herself once again, relishing being single. The commitment for this courageous Brit was truly "keep calm and carry on."*

Maintaining identity within every relationship is at the heart of healthy singleness. Those in love relationships who lose sight of this often forfeit the qualities that attracted their mate and drain the wellspring of their love. Much of the pain of divorce comes from the struggle to gain back this identity. Singleness is not a selfish stand independent of others. It's a "self-full" attitude, a belief in one's worthiness supported by healthy behavior that enriches all relationships.

The Individual Self and the Relationship Self

Here's a fundamental paradox about relationships:

- To be in a good relationship of any kind, you must know yourself.
- You cannot fully know yourself until you are in a close friendship or love relationship.

We grow as we interact, and that interaction is enhanced by the growth we make as individuals. This interplay between the development of the individual self and the development of the relationship self has two important principles:

1. The relationship with another person will not take care of the relationship with yourself.
2. When not in a close relationship, personal growth will *not* provide you with all that it takes to resolve the challenges that will arise in a future relationship.

Your intimate relationship self goes dormant when you become single after divorce. Close friendships and family relationships can approximate many of the intimate interactions of a love relationship. However, it's in the context of a committed love relationship—where there is unique physical, emotional, intellectual, and spiritual intimacy—that you experience your deepest committed relationship self. When your relationship self does reemerge in another love relationship, leftovers from previous partnerships will arise that must be dealt with to create a healthier union. Until that time, develop your individual self through singleness and friendships. Acquire new relationship skills. When with a new love partner, use these skills to help evolve your relationship self.

Singleness does not mean isolating yourself as often happens during the first stages of loss. Even when there's no long-term commitment, you still learn important lessons about yourself from connections with others. In what Fisher and Alberti call "relatedness," you can sample intellectual, emotional, and physical intimacy. You can also practice open communication and explore authentic, here-and-now involvement.

Relatedness—Growing Relationships That Heal

Relationship Types

Recognizing relationship types can help you make choices about connecting. Here are four major types (Gorski 1993, 91–97):

Trial dating relationships. These assist in learning about your responses. This is especially important if you historically haven't dated much. In a limited way, this behavior can be enjoyed with platonic friends. (See chapter 15, on building friendships.)

Transitional relationships. These are short-term connections that meet immediate needs, such as support, sex, tenderness. These are the "growing relationships" Fisher and Alberti discuss and can include platonic friends as well as romantic partners depending on needs met. They occur between the lonely and painful stages of divorce recovery and the healthy search for a long-term partner. These can be satisfying when both partners communicate and meet expectations and needs, including honesty about termination.

Short-term physical intimacy. These relationships may range from one-night stands to several weeks. After divorce, these can be anonymous outlets for sexual experimentation. One may never choose this because it goes against values.

Committed relationship. This a long-term, monogamous connection where both partners get deepest needs met over an open-ended period of time.

You may alternate between these relationship types. For example, you could begin with nonsexual transitional relationships with friends until you have the strength and healing to branch out into trial dating. Short-term physical intimacy may be an option, especially when you use protection against disease and see this type of connection for what it is. After significant healing, you may choose a committed relationship again using new knowledge and maturity.

Explore your current attitudes about these relationship types. Review this assessment in the future to see if your attitudes have changed.

1. Trial dating relationships
    Reasons for: _____

    Reasons against: _____

2. Transitional relationships

Reasons for: _____

Reasons against: _____

3. Short-term physical intimacy
Reasons for: _____

Reasons against: _____

4. Committed relationships
Reasons for: _____

Reasons against: _____

What did you find that surprised you? _____

What will you choose now? _____

In this stage, you may find partners who are unsuitable for a long-term relationship. That's okay. This has nothing to do with either person's worthiness. Growing relationships are

most often short term. Also, be wary of emotionally investing in dead-end partnerships:
- A passionate affair can burn itself out in a few months and is inevitably closed-ended.
- One partner who is more invested in the relationship than the other person and is readily available for sex, companionship, and relating. Unequal involvement ensures a lack of commitment. You could wind up in either role.
- Getting involved with someone who is already in a committed relationship. This may set "safe" limits, yet it can also foster heartache, loss, and value conflicts.
- Living together may be a way to relate without commitment. However, incompatible living habits, money issues, career, and family still intrude. Those who live together compatibly also have no guarantee that commitment or marriage would be successful.

Fisher and Alberti give guidelines to prepare for moving on from your growing relationship:

- Maintain open and honest communication, especially about feelings and needs.
- Live in the present rather than fantasize about a future.
- Don't play games about the reality of your relationship.
- Plan for termination with arrangements around money, housing, mutual friends.
- Discuss desires about continuing a friendship after the love relationship ends.

Characteristics and Values About Dating

As you did with sexuality, compile a list of attitudes about dating behavior. Use these to measure the quality of your dating experiences and manage your behavior and expectations. Be mindful of platonic connections as well as romantic ones. (Do more as you can.)

Satisfying dating activity ought to involve:

1. _____
2. _____
3. _____
4. _____
5. _____
6. _____

Overall, what emerges as your core value in dating?

1. _____
2. _____

Listen to the Healthy Dating visualization (available at http://www.newharbinger.com/45397) to envision success in relatedness.

Intimacy is at the heart of mating. More than sexual union for pleasure or procreation, mating is the choice to spend major parts of one's life in a love relationship with the goal of ongoing companionship—the comfortable, safe place where one exchanges deep vulnerabilities and meets needs, feeling accepted and loved within a commitment of mutually satisfying involvement. The next section will help you understand different relationship types and your pathway to making healthier choices to express and experience love.

Choosing Love

Your ideals, expectations, and behaviors helped create your relationships. (Review your work on the ideal image in chapter 7.) Understand these characteristics, realize alternatives, and make new choices to build the healthier relationships you deserve. Let's start by defining "love" and what being "in love" is for you. Use all five freedoms—your sensory experience, thoughts and feelings that accompany it, the desires that are fulfilled, and the behaviors you engage in.
1. "Love" is: _____
2. The experience of being "in love" includes: _____
    Physical relating (sensory experience): _____

    Thoughts: _____

    Feelings: _____

Desires fulfilled: _____

Your behavior: _____

What you've just described is more than the emotional experience of love. It's a powerful, often subconscious motivator—your "blueprint" for finding a mate. This blueprint may limit how you interpret relationships so alternatives, even healthier ones, may be overlooked. Also, when you experience some of these qualities with a potential partner, it's quite easy to assume that other qualities will be met by this person whether or not that's true. Rather than relying on a possibly unrealistic, unhealthy ideal, make conscious your choices about love and mating. To understand the range of alternatives, let's examine what's been called "the styles of loving."

The Styles of Loving

The styles of loving were derived from the pioneering work of Canadian sociologist John Lee (Fisher and Alberti

2016). They represent choices to love and accept love in distinct ways. The following are my descriptions of the six different styles.

1. Best friends:
    - Common interests.
    - Companions.
    - "Growing in love" rather than "falling in love."
    - Even-ness of temperament, steady commitment, stable interactions.
    - Conflict resolved rationally.
    - Steadfast loyalty.
    - Ex-partners often remain friends.
2. Game-playing:
    - Love as a game; game player enjoys the "chase."
    - Avoidance of real intimacy through deceit, multiple partners, or self-centered self-sufficiency.
    - Faked involvement.
    - Unattached, uninvolved, and distant.
3. Practical:
    - Practicality is most important.
    - Logical love choices for compatibility concerning financial,

career, family, education, religion, appearance, personality, and so forth.
- Emotional involvement comes after practical considerations are satisfied.
4. Needy:
- Can be addicted to beloved, desiring both to possess and be possessed.
- Intense involvement.
- Extreme emotional or physical dependency.
- Demanding needs for attention.
- Codependency, losing identity in another.
- Manipulativeness and jealousy; relationship endings can be explosive and bitter.
5. Romantic:
- Intense desire for physical and emotional involvement and merging.
- Passion is essential.
- Separation is insufferable.
- Love of loving.
6. Altruistic:
- Values beloved's needs and desires above everything else.

- Love is sacrifice of self for another.
- Compassion and understanding for partner's shortcomings.
- In the extreme, unselfish lover very "other-directed" (meeting the partner's needs as primary way to meet one's own); reciprocity not necessary.

By examining your ended relationship, you find whether or not your style, the partner you chose, and the relationship you created was healthy and met your needs. Become aware of your behavior and reinforce what's positive and change what doesn't work. Clinging to old patterns will only create more of the same. Reexamine your definition of love and your description of being "in love," then answer the following:

What characteristics of your definitions fit which style(s) of loving? _____
_____
_____

What thoughts and feelings does this bring up? _____

What was your style(s) in your ended relationship? _____

What behaviors lead to this conclusion? _____

What was your ex-partner's style(s)? _____

What behaviors lead to this conclusion? _____

What thoughts, feelings, and desires do these answers bring up? _____

How might this change your intentions and actions for the future? _____

Will's Take Patricia found stable, respectful men "boring." She kept falling "head over heels" in love with *game-players who physically abused and dumped her. When friends pointed out her folly, she'd say, "But I love him!" Unless she changes her style of loving, she's doomed to intense, painful, and unfulfilling love relationships.*

Perhaps a blend of styles, such as the following, makes the most sense. Being best friends with your love partner can be the foundation. This can include romance as well as being practical with money, career, and family. There are times when sacrifice is appropriate, so altruism has a place. Small amounts of game-playing may add spice as a dash of pepper gives taste to a meal. The loyalty of a committed relationship retains a treasured belongingness that is reminiscent of neediness. *All of these behaviors must be balanced within a framework of healthy intimacy wherein each partner respects self as well as each other.* This may be what you've been seeking all along.

Balance comes from knowing what you want and communicating it as well as attending to your partner's appropriate needs and desires. As you relate, you're constantly teaching your partner who you are and what you want by what you say, and most importantly, what you do and the behavior you accept. You're also learning about your partner as he or she does the same. Simply saying, "I feel loved when...", or "I don't feel loved (respected, listened to, honored) when..." allows you to be yourself as you share with others. It also helps you evaluate the depth of your connection by your partner's responses. Make lists of behavior: what is loving for you and behavior that is not loving. These can prepare you for clear communication and evaluation in any type of relationship. Examples:

- I feel loved when you give me a backrub when I ask for it.
- I don't feel loved when you tell me not to feel a certain way.

Loving Behavior List

I feel loved when:

1. _____
2. _____
3. _____
4. _____
5. _____
6. _____

Unloving Behavior List
I don't feel love when:

1. _____
2. _____
3. _____
4. _____
5. _____
6. _____

Your reactions to these lists: _____

Expand these lists. They'll assist you in building healthy dating relationships. Sharing them with a love partner will build intimacy, respect, and clarity. Listen to the Healthy Love Relationship visualization (available at http://www.newharbinger.com/45397) to guide you.

Journaling to Freedom

Write a letter to your future love partner declaring your intentions to remain a loving, caring individual, able to be intimate in a healthy give-and-take relationship.

_____
_____
_____
_____
_____
_____
_____

Your strength of heart is reflected in the life you lead. Acceptance of life's abundance brings you to the next chapter, on purpose, almost at the summit of the rebuilding block mountain.

Action Steps for Moving Onward

Sharing with trusted family, friends, and dating partners deepens intimacy.

1. Write out your current and future lists for activities of interest. Take the ones you choose and enjoy developing them.

2. Evaluate the reasons for and against the different relationship types.

3. Distill your values about dating by listing beliefs and behaviors.

4. Listen to the Healthy Dating visualization (downloadable audio).

5. Define "love" and "in love."

6. Determine your style of loving and that of your ex-partner. Evaluate and respond to these answers.

7. Fill out lists of behaviors for "I feel loved when..." and "I don't feel loved when..."

8. Listen to the Healthy Love Relationship visualization (downloadable audio).

9. Listen to I Am Moving On meditation (downloadable audio).

10. Write your letter to your future love partner.

11. Be purposeful in caring for yourself. Make this a habit.

Part VI

Reaching Wholeness

Reaching the top of the rebuilding block mountain is both an end and a beginning. You complete your divorce journey and find other peaks to scale in your future. The strength and knowledge you've gained gives you fortitude to face life with courage, skill, and enthusiasm. The last two chapters prepare you to move forward with awareness of your growth, aimed toward the rewarding future you so richly deserve.

Chapter 18 will help you discover what you've gained going through your journey of recovery from relationship loss. It shapes purpose through questions about your future and guides you toward deeper connections with self and others.

Chapter 19 completes your healing journey up the rebuilding blocks by helping you realize your inner strengths and make choices about your new freedom.

Chapter 18

Purpose: Accepting Abundance for the Journey Onward

...loss constitutes an odd kind of fullness; despair empties out into an unquenchable appetite for life.
—Gretel Ehrlich

STEPS ALONG THE WAY

1. **Discovering the Gains from Your Loss**
2. **Purpose—Questions for Your Future**
3. **Building Deep Connections Within and Without**

An end is always a beginning. Your new life and the love you choose begin with the ending of your love relationship and letting go of the person you were. *Who you are now is formed by the decisions you've made and your growth through this loss.* The changes in your world are extensions of your transformation. As you reach the top of the rebuilding block mountain, other journeys beckon. *Who you become will be created by the decisions you make right now.* None of these decisions will be more important than accepting the abundance life offers.

The core of divorce recovery is life recovery, so be aware of what you've learned and be open to exploration. Accepting abundance allows you to accomplish this by:
1. Acknowledging the benefits that relationship loss has brought you
2. Framing the next steps in your journey of life—your purpose
3. Building deeper connections.

Discovering the Gains from Your Loss

Even if emotional pain reappears, acknowledge the positive lessons you've learned. This reinforces a willingness to grow in every situation. Rate the following on a scale of 1 (low) to 10 (high) to indicate the strength of each quality now, after your work on healing from relationship loss. Note how you've thrived because of your healing work. Add to this list, and come back to it regularly to see how your rankings change over time and your continued growth.

1. Authentic	
2. Aware of emotions	
3. Self-esteem and self-confidence	
4. Assertive	
5. Sense of identity	
6. Manage anger	
7. Self-love	
8. Positive friendships	
9. Understand intimacy	
10. Nurture self	
11. Change effects of upbringing	
12. Overcome loneliness	
13. Grieve to relieve sorrow	
14. Fear as positive motivator	
15. Forgive self and others	
16. Positive self-image	
17. Sexuality awareness	
18. Understand and communicate love	
19.	
20.	

Journaling to Freedom

Compose a letter of thankfulness. This can be addressed to you, your former love partner, a friend, or whomever. Recognize how your healing process has brought you a sense of abundance through acquired wisdom about yourself and life.

Dear _____,

_____
_____
_____
_____
_____
_____
_____
_____

New worlds open up, none greater than the one inside you.

Purpose—Questions for Your Future

As you climb closer to the top of the rebuilding blocks, many questions remain (Fisher and Alberti 2016). Your answers are the leading edge of your willingness to accept abundance. Proclaim your ability to meet these challenges and reinforce your confidence that life will give what you need to thrive, not just survive.

1. What is success for you? Be specific. Describe the ideal outcome.

   a. Personal: _____
   _____
   _____

   b. Family: _____
   _____
   _____

   c. Friends, neighbors, coworkers: _____
   _____
   _____

   d. Dating and relationship partners: _____
   _____
   _____

   e. Career: _____
   _____
   _____

2. What conditions bring security? _____

3. What contributes to self-esteem? ____

4. What's necessary to experience happiness? ____

With these answers in mind, make specific goals, ones you're willing to strive to achieve.

Short-Term Goals

Short-term goals are where you want to be in the next month, three months, or six months. Look at your answers to the questions for the challenge aspect of self-love in chapter 14 for ideas.

1. Relationship with yourself (diet, exercise, education): ____

2. Relationships with family (children, parents, siblings): ____

3. Relationships with friends, neighbors, coworkers: _____

4. Relationships with dating partners: _____

5. Career: _____

6. Relationship with life in general: _____

Intermediate Goals

Intermediate goals indicate where you want to be in the next year to three years to get you closer to your ideals.

1. Relationship with yourself (diet, exercise, education): _____

2. Relationships with family (children, parents, siblings): _____

3. Relationships with friends, neighbors, coworkers: _____

4. Relationships with dating partners: _____

5. Career: _____

6. Relationship with life in general: _____

Long-Range Goals
   Long-range goals indicate where you want to be in five years. Hopefully, these are close to your ideals. Review and assess to determine. These answers will change as you do. Return to them to see progress and refine. Develop this blueprint for who you are and who you

want to become. Life goes by too quickly not to make purposeful choices. (Review the method on working backward from your goal in chapter 3.)

Finally, know that those who live to the fullest are those who release those thoughts, feelings, and attachments that no longer serve them. This will open you up to the freedom discussed the next chapter. What do you need to let go?

1. Relationship with yourself (diet, exercise, education): _____

   _____

   _____

2. Relationships with family (children, parents, siblings): _____

   _____

   _____

3. Relationships with friends, neighbors, coworkers: _____

   _____

   _____

4. Relationships with dating partners: _____

   _____

   _____

5. Career: _____

6. Relationship with life in general: _____

Building Deep Connections Within and Without

Knowing our deepest self, the essential self, will inevitably take us from inner connection to a thirst for connecting with others.

Connecting with the Essential Self

We are born with our essence as human beings, and we leave this life stripped of everything except that essence. In the time between these two awesome events, it is our choice either to realize this essential spirit or to live in ignorance of its grace and serenity. The recovery of this consciousness helps us assume our birthright: a life of joy and wholeness.

We discussed the essential self in chapters 11 and 13. What holds you back from this inner connection?

Obstacles to Awareness of the Essential Self

Evaluate on a scale of 1 (low obstacle) to 10 (high obstacle).

Not healed from shaming influences. Family of origin and subsequent shaming relationships still effect self-image. This keeps a person stuck in codependency, masks, and roles.	Rating: _____
Maintain lack of responsibility for self. Unaware of basic worth and strengths, it becomes easy to blame others for unhappiness instead of choosing the path of recovery.	Rating: _____
Unawareness that we're linked to life and cocreate our lives through that bond. Without recognizing this connection, our choices prevent us from experiencing abundance.	Rating: _____

What do you need to do? _____

What will you do about it? _____

Connectedness to Creation

Discover yourself in a benevolent world. Go beyond divorce recovery to where the original five freedoms flower into being connected within, with your essential self, and with all life. Recall the layers we've looked at:

| Original Five Freedoms: | Sense Awareness | Thoughts | Feelings | Wants & Needs | Behavior Choice |

Family neglect or abuse brings:

| Effects of Shame: | Non-Sense | False Self | Frozen Feelings | Lost Self | Masked Self |

Healing and authenticity brings:

| Healthy Responsibility: | Open to the World | Transforming Thoughts | Freeing All Feelings | Integration of Wants & Needs | Living Consciously |

Now, we'll add this final layer of healing:

| Connectedness to Life: | Sempathy | Inner Voice | Serenity & Enthusiasm | Desire to Relate | Balanced Life of Love |

1. Sense Awareness Becomes Sempathy

"Sempathy" is a word I coined from a combination of "sense" and "empathy." It's a physically felt connectedness to creation. We become aware of the world and others through our five senses of sight, hearing, touch, taste, and smell. This physical experience leads us to identify with another and understand how it must be for that person.

For example, a good friend shares with you how he or she was verbally abused by a spouse. You see your friend's red eyes and face and hear the hurt and anger in your friend's voice. You may have had a similar experience and feel the outrage your friend is communicating.

Never assume your sempathy is the true reality of someone else. Communicate to find out his or her experience. Also, sempathy ought never to replace how your sensory experience affects you, otherwise you might attend to another's reality before your own.

2. Thought Becomes Listening to Your Inner Voice

Beyond conscious interpretation, this unique voice connects you to your essential self. It can help you determine how to live and how to relate. *(Trust this voice only when you've removed shaming childhood messages and feel a peaceful confidence.)* Finding, listening, and believing the wisdom of your inner voice is a strong statement of your recovery and self-acceptance.

Will's Take *My inner voice speaks calmly, lovingly, without anxiety. When I'm stressed, the chatter in my brain can drown out my reasonable inner voice. When I allow this chatter, my decisions are not as good as they could have been.*

3. Feelings Become Serenity and Enthusiasm

When connected with others sempathically and with your inner voice, an amazing mixture of excitement and contentment results.

Serenity is living relatively free from inner strife where your calm mind and open heart perceive and experience life for what it is, not for what you might wish it to be. It helps you live without forcing things to change. Serenity allows you to value the preciousness of life and accept the appreciation that life offers you.

Enthusiasm is an eagerness for life. It propels you to live to the fullest with the passion of being involved, to partake of life in large delicious bites because all of us are meant to *live,* not merely exist.

4. Wants Become a Desire to Relate

When you feel calm and live fully and clearly, a desire to relate on many levels is reborn. This ranges from friendships to love relationships. Breaking free from toxic shame allows you to perceive and accept your fundamental goodness. You become eager to share this in involvement with others' fundamental goodness.

5. Behavior Becomes a Balanced Life of Love

With a healthier self who desires to connect with healthy others, you move toward to a balanced life of love. By definition, balance is not this or that but a combination of both. It's constructed of elements combined into a harmonious whole. What makes your life balanced is the awareness of yourself, others, and your surroundings while understanding *and respecting* the boundaries between them.

Here, love is behavior that values life, such as saying no to a loved one to value your needs and at other times, saying yes when that's appropriate. Flexibility is key because different situations influence how you choose to express your value of life.

Connectedness is always present. What you're working on is your conscious awareness and practice of it. Assess your level of connectedness. Rate on a scale of 1 (low) to 10 (high).

1. *Sempathy.* You are able to sense and feel empathy for others. You connect with others, but don't let this influence your involvement in your own life. When appropriate, you check out your felt experience.	Rating: _____
2. *Listening to your inner voice.* You take time to quiet down and hear its message. You act on its advice and find its assistance invaluable.	Rating: _____
3. *Serenity and enthusiasm.* You cope with the complications of living while retaining excitement about your new life. You have an underlying peacefulness, knowing that you're okay.	Rating: _____
4. *Desire to relate.* You establish good family connections and friendships. You're open to the possibility of a love relationship.	Rating: _____
5. *Balanced life of love.* You relate with supportive family and friends and expand social horizons. You have a deep reservoir of love and acceptance for the abundance of life wherever you are and in whatever you're doing.	Rating: _____

Your reaction: _____

Use the Accepting Abundance visualization (available at http://www.newharbinger.com/45397) to accept abundance and build your new life.

Journaling to Freedom

Write a letter to the universe proclaiming your willingness and ability to accept abundance in all its forms. Realize your strength to be who you really are.

Dear Universe,

_____
_____
_____
_____
_____
_____
_____

In the next chapter you'll arrive at the summit of the rebuilding block mountain. This symbolizes the freedom to live the life you choose. You can see the path you climbed and the obstacles you overcame. From there, you can step more confidently into a future of new challenges, one you are prepared to begin.

Action Steps for Moving Onward

As always, share and discuss these results with supportive others.

1. Assess the benefits of divorce recovery.
2. Write your letter of thankfulness.
3. Answer the questions for your future.
4. List those thoughts, feelings, and attachments you are ready to let go.
5. Assess your obstacles to inner connectedness.
6. Assess your expression of the five freedoms through connectedness to life.
7. Listen to the Accepting Abundance visualization (downloadable audio) at least three times this week.
8. Listen to the Now I Understand meditation (downloadable audio).
9. Write your letter to the universe.
10. Do something memorable to celebrate your completion of this workbook.

Chapter 19

Freedom, the View from the Mountaintop

Some men see things as they are, and ask why. I dream of things that never were, and ask why not.
—Robert F. Kennedy

STEPS ALONG THE WAY

1. **Realizing Your Strengths**
2. **Choosing Your Freedom**

The clear air is cool, crisp, refreshing. The mountain peak that seemed so distant when you began your climb is now at your feet. Take a deep breath. This is what freedom feels like. Though your gaze may aim at the mountains and valleys ahead of you, turn around and look back. See what you've accomplished. It's amazing.

Realizing Your Strengths

Though it's been difficult at times, you've climbed the rebuilding blocks. Recognize what your healing journey says about you. Here are just a few:

- You're *courageous* in your willingness to face your fears, overcome loneliness, and express grief and anger.
- You have *perseverance* to do what it takes not just what feels good.
- You have *curiosity* to discover the patterns that work and the ones that don't as well as the *toughness* to change.
- You have shown *discipline* in your efforts to understand your life and make better choices.
- You have *compassion* for yourself and others as you seek to become a better friend.
- You have shown *love* in how you've come to change how you relate to self and others.
- You are *trustworthy* in how you strive to be *intimate* and honest with others.
- You are *purposeful* in your growth.

- And, you realize that you're *worthy* to be alive, worthy to have the freedom to choose to love and live, and worthy of all the good things life has to offer.

Celebrate these and the many other qualities you have discovered and enhanced in your healing journey up this mountain.

Choosing Your Freedom

Freedom can mean many things. Perhaps now that you've reached this mountaintop, it means something different for you than it did before. Take a few moments and reflect.

What does freedom mean to you?

_____
_____
_____

What will you do with this freedom?

_____
_____
_____

If you could, what words of wisdom or encouragement would you give to the "you" of the past, who stood at the foot of this mountain, wondering if you could make this journey?

_____

_____

What words of encouragement do you have for yourself now as you embark on your life after relationship loss?

_____

_____

Finally, consider this old Irish prayer whose author is unknown:

> *Take time to work, it is the price of success.*
> *Take time to think, it is the source of power.*
> *Take time to play, it is the secret to perpetual youth.*
> *Take time to read, it is the foundation of wisdom.*
> *Take time to be friendly, it is the road to happiness.*
> *Take time to dream, it is hitching your wagon to a star.*

Take time to love and be loved, it is the privilege of the gods.
Take time to look around, the day is too short to be selfish.
Take time to laugh, it is the music of the soul.

Will's Take THANK YOU so much for the opportunity to encourage you on your climb up the rebuilding blocks. The fact that you've gone through this workbook shows how much you believe in yourself. I am awed by your courage and fortitude.

Though you may need to revisit this workbook to complete leftover thoughts, feelings, and actions in your recovery from relationship loss, celebrate your accomplishment of reaching this place at this time. As you tackle leftover issues, know that you are courageously working on what you need to do. There's no timetable for completion. Your success is evident in your daily efforts to become a healthier person.

This peak at the top of the rebuilding blocks is but one of many summits on your journey through life. As you step into your future, know that you are indeed a unique marvel of creation. Be kind to yourself and your world. All will be well.

Welcome to Your New Life!

Afterword

by Nina Hart-Fisher

As I wrote in the introduction, this updated *Rebuilding Workbook* is a long-time dream fully realized.

In all the years teaching with Bruce, we were truly fortunate to learn about character and choice from so many courageous and authentic people. Two memories come to mind:

- John, the Australian man who discovered his purpose was to live a life of growth. When he shared, Bruce and I smiled knowingly at each other, silently agreeing that growing is what life is all about.
- Bridgette, a lovely Canadian woman who cried as she gave thanks for the seminar. Bruce and I also knew that gratitude is essential for personal growth along with compassion, honesty, trust, humor, and love, always love.

One of our favorite books was the *Velveteen Rabbit* by Margery Williams, a sweet story about a stuffed toy bunny brought to life through the love of a little boy. While I was pregnant with our son Robert, Bruce and I often pondered whether nestled inside every human heart lives a tiny child simply desiring to love that much. Now that I am seventy-three, I think perhaps there is!

Here is my sincere wish for you, courageous reader. May you be both the child and the bunny—to love and be loved—the most powerful force in the universe. All my best on your journey of healing, growing, and loving. BE WELL.

Acknowledgments

Will—

I want to thank Norm Gibson, LCSW, former director of the Rebuilding Seminars, for his friendship, support, and kindness in giving feedback for this book. I also want to thank Nick Meima, MA, founder of AfterDivorceSupport.com and coordinator of Rebuilding.org, and Deb Azorsky, MA, for their observations and feedback, and Jay Wolf for his scale to measure disentanglement.

Special thanks to Dan Doyle, PhD, for his creative critiquing, astute comments, and steady assistance.

His support was invaluable.

I am grateful to Anna-Maria Crum for her artistry of the mask illustrations.

I have special appreciation for Nina Hart-Fisher, my contributor for this workbook. Her insight, suggestions, and encouragement were indispensable. She is a special person in my life, so caring, a great friend and laughing partner.

Most importantly, my deep love and appreciation goes to my wife, Catherine, for her patience and for loving me in so many ways, surprising me each day.

Nina—

To my beloved husband, Dr. Bruce Fisher, the love of my life, my best friend, supportive stepfather to my two daughters, and phenomenal father to our son, Dr. Robert W. Hart Fisher. I am truly blessed to have known you and loved you.

To Will Limón, with profound gratitude for making this updated *Rebuilding Workbook* informative and relevant for the twenty-first century. I think it's outstanding.

To you, the reader. I celebrate your commitment and courage to rebuild yourself and your life.

We both thank Robert Alberti for the foreword and his support. We also thank Tesilya Hanauer and Caleb Beckwith. You helped keep this project on track. We truly appreciate the care and manner in which you presented ideas and suggestions.

Our thanks as well to Gretel Hakanson for her expert copyediting.

References

Alberti, R., and M. Emmons. 2017. *Your Perfect Right: Assertiveness and Equality in Your Life and Relationships,* 10th ed. Oakland, CA: Impact Publishers.

Berne, E. 2010. *Games People Play.* New York: Penguin.

Bradshaw, J. 2005. *Healing the Shame That Binds You,* rev. ed. Deerfield Beach, FL: Health Communications, Inc.

Burkan, T., and P.D. Burkan. 1983. *Guiding Yourself into a Spiritual Reality,* rev. ed. Twain Heart, CA: Reunion Press, Inc.

Callahan, B.N. 1979. *Separation and Divorce.* New York: Family Service Association of America.

Cooley, M.L., and J.G. Hollandsworth. 1977. "A Strategy for Teaching Verbal Content of Assertive Responses" in *Assertiveness: Innovations, Applications,*

Issues, ed. R.E. Alberti. San Luis Obispo, CA: Impact Publishers.

Davis, M., E.R. Eshelman, and M. McKay. 2008. *The Relaxation and Stress Reduction Workbook,* 6th ed. Oakland, CA: New Harbinger Publications, Inc.

Dyer, W. 2001. *Pulling Your Own Strings,* reprint ed. New York: William Morrow Paperbacks.

Ellis, A. 1975. *A New Guide to Rational Living.* North Hollywood, CA: Wilshire Books.

Fisher, B., and N. Hart-Fisher. 2000. *Loving Choices, 2nd ed.* Oakland, CA: Impact Publishers.

Fisher, B., and N. Hart-Fisher. 2000. *Loving Choices Workbook.* Oakland, CA: Impact Publishers.

Fisher, B., and R. Alberti. 2016. *Rebuilding: When Your Relationship Ends,* 4th ed. Oakland, CA: Impact Publishers.

Forsyth, J., and G. Eifert. 2016. *The Mindfulness and Acceptance Workbook for Anxiety,* 2nd ed. Oakland, CA: New Harbinger Publications, Inc.

Gordon, T. 2008. *PET: Parent Effectiveness Training,* 30th ed. New York: Three Rivers Press.

Gorski, T. 1993. *Getting Love Right: Learning the Choices of Healthy Intimacy.* New York: Fireside/Parkside.

Gračanin, A., A.J.J.M. Vingerhoets, I Kardum, M. Zupčić, M. Šantek, and M. Šimić. 2015. "Why Crying Does and Sometimes Does Not Seem to Alleviate Mood: A Quasi-Experimental Study." *Motivation and Emotion* 39: 953–960.

Harris, T. 2012. *I'm OK—You're OK.* London, UK: Arrow.

Hendricks, G. 2016. *Learning to Love Yourself.* Seattle: Amazon.

Johns Hopkins. 2010. "Children Who Lose a Parent to Suicide More Likely to Die the Same Way." *Johns Hopkins*

News and Publications. https://www.hopkinsmedicine.org/news/media/releases/children_who_lose_a_parent_to_suicide_more_likely_to_die_the_same_way.

Langelier, C.A., and J.D. Connell. 2005. "Emotions and Learning: Where Brain-Based Research and Cognitive-Behavioral Counseling Strategies Meet the Road." *Rivier College Online Academic Journal* 1(1): 1–13.

Leahy, R., D. Tirch, and L. Napolitano. 2011. *Emotion Regulation in Psychotherapy: A Practitioner's Guide.* New York: Guildford Press.

Leahy, R. 2020. *Don't Believe Everything You Feel: A CBT Workbook to Identify Your Emotional Schemas and Find Freedom from Anxiety and Depression.* Oakland, CA: New Harbinger Publications, Inc.

Limón, W. 2016. *Beyond the End of Love: Beginning Again After Relationship Loss.* Seattle: Amazon.

Limón, W., and K. Whalen. 1986. *The Roots of Love: Living from the Heart.* Loveland, CO: Health Promotion.

Madow, L. 1972. *Anger: How to Recognize and Cope with It.* New York: Macmillan Publishing Company.

Maslow, A. 2013. *A Theory of Human Motivation,* reprint of original 1943 edition. Jersey City, NJ: Start Publishing, LLC.

Masters, W., V. Johnson, and R. Kolodny. 1988. *Masters and Johnson on Sex and Human Loving.* New York: Little, Brown, and Company.

McGill, M. 1986. *The McGill Report on Male Intimacy.* New York: Perennial Library.

McKay, M., M. Davis, and P. Fanning. 2011. *Thoughts & Feelings: Taking Control of Your Moods & Your Life,* 4th ed. Oakland, CA: New Harbinger Publications, Inc.

McKay, M., P. Rogers, and J. McKay. 2003. *When Anger Hurts,* 2nd ed. Oakland, CA: New Harbinger Publications, Inc.

McKay, M., J. Wood, and J. Brantley. 2007. *The Dialectical Behavior Therapy Skills Workbook.* Oakland, CA: New Harbinger Publications, Inc.

Moustakas, C.E. 1972. *Loneliness and Love.* Englewood Cliffs, NJ: Prentice-Hall, Inc.

Murray, W.H. 1951. *The Scottish Himalayan Expedition.* London: J.M. Dent & Sons.

Narang, D. 2014. *Loneliness: A Workbook: Building Relationships with Yourself and Others.* Encino, CA: Stronger Relationships.

Nhat Hanh, T. 2016. "How to Release Anger Through Mindfulness." *Uplift* (May 31). https://upliftconnect.com/release-anger-mindfulness/.

Pam, N. 2018. "Denial of Reality (Denial)." Psychology Dictionary. https://psychologydictionary.org/denial-of-reality-denial/.

Perry, B., and M. Szalavitz. 2010. *Born for Love: Why Empathy Is Essential—and Endangered.* New York: William Morrow.

Peck, M.S. 1978. *The Road Less Traveled.* New York: Simon & Schuster.

Potter-Efron, R., and P. Potter-Efron. 2006. *Letting Go of Anger,* 2nd ed. Oakland, CA: New Harbinger Publications, Inc.

Powell, J. 1995. *Unconditional Love.* Chicago: Thomas More Association.

Powell, J. 1999. *Why Am I Afraid to Tell You Who I Am?* Grand Rapids, MI: Zondervan.

Rilke, R.M., trans K.W. Maurer. 1943. *Letters to a Young Poet.* London: Langley & Sons, Ltd. The Euston Press, N.W.I.

Ryan, R., and E. Deci. 2018. *Self-Determination Theory: Basic Psychological Needs in Motivation, Development, and Wellness.* New York: Guilford Press.

Satir, V. 1995. *Making Contact.* Berkeley, CA: Celestial Arts.

Seltzer, L. 2013. "Anger: How We Transfer Feelings of Guilt, Hurt, and Fear." *Psychology Today.* https://www.psychologytoday.com/us/blog/evolution-the-self/201306/anger-how-we-transfer-feelings-guilt-hurt-and-fear.

Stromberg, J. 2013. "The Microscopic Structure of Dried Human Tears." *Smithsonian* (November 13). https://www.smithsonianmag.com/science-nature/the-microscopic-structures-of-dried-human-tears-180947766/?no-ist.

Vilhauer, J. 2015. "3 Simple Steps to Control Anger and Frustration with Others." *Psychology Today.* https://www.psychologytoday.com/us/blog/living-forward/201504/3-simple-steps-control-anger-and-frustration-others.

Will Limón, MSW, is an educator, counselor, and author who worked directly with Bruce Fisher, coauthor of *Rebuilding*. For more than twenty years, he presented the Rebuilding Seminar on divorce recovery, and for forty years presented his own programs on relationships, communication, and energetic healing to thousands of participants. He is author of several books, including the internationally published *Beginning Again*.

Nina Hart-Fisher is a PhD candidate in psychology, focusing on children of divorce. She co-led educational seminars internationally with her late husband, Bruce Fisher, for two decades. She is coauthor of *Loving Choices,* also with Bruce Fisher. After nearly fifty years living in Boulder, CO, Nina now resides in Maui, HI.

Foreword writer **Robert Alberti, PhD,** has received international recognition for his writing and editing, often praised as the "gold standard" for psychological self-help. Alberti's "formal" publications career began in 1970, with the first edition of *Your Perfect Right,* coauthored with Michael Emmons. Alberti collaborated with the late divorce therapist Bruce Fisher on the third edition of *Rebuilding,* and recently completed the revised fourth edition.

MORE BOOKS from NEW HARBINGER PUBLICATIONS

REBUILDING, FOURTH EDITION
When Your Relationship Ends

Impact Publishers
An Imprint of New Harbinger Publications

CO-PARENTING WITH A TOXIC EX
What to Do When Your Ex-Spouse Tries to Turn the Kids Against You

WIRED FOR DATING
How Understanding Neurobiology & Attachment Style Can Help You Find Your Ideal Mate

TAKING SEXY BACK
How to Own Your Sexuality & Create the Relationships You Want

THE BLINDSPOTS BETWEEN US
How to Overcome Unconscious Cognitive Bias & Build Better Relationships

ANXIETY HAPPENS
52 Ways to Find Peace of Mind

newharbingerpublications
1-800-748-6273 / newharbinger.com

(VISA, MC, AMEX / prices subject to change without notice)
Follow Us

Don't miss out on new books in the subjects that interest you.
Sign up for our **Book Alerts** at **newharbinger.com/bookalerts**

Back Cover Material

Are you ready to rebuild?

If you're going through a painful breakup or divorce, you may feel like the life you once knew is crashing down around you. You need help gathering the pieces and "rebuilding" yourself from the ground up. Based on the #1 trusted resource on divorce recovery, *Rebuilding,* this workbook offers step-by-step guidance to help you put your life back together when a relationship ends.

With this powerful and practical guide, you'll work through grief and anger, overcome the fear of being alone, and learn to establish a new sense of identity. You'll understand how to forgive yourself and others, set healthy boundaries, and explore new relationships. Also, you'll discover a proven approach for healing called *the divorce process rebuilding blocks*—a set of tools to help you and your kids manage and minimize the trauma that can occur when a relationship ends. A breakup can feel as painful as the death of a loved one. But by using the rebuilding blocks to recovery outlined in this workbook, you'll find the courage to let go of your old life and embrace the new you.

Based on the #1 trusted resource on divorce recovery, *Rebuilding*

***

WILL LIMÓN, MSW, is an educator, counselor, and author of several books, including the internationally published *Beginning Again.* He worked directly with Bruce Fisher, coauthor of *Rebuilding,* and presented the Rebuilding Seminar on divorce recovery for more than twenty years.

NINA HART-FISHER is a PhD candidate in psychology, focusing on children of divorce. She co-led educational seminars internationally with her late husband, Bruce Fisher, for two decades. Nina fully embraces the Aloha Spirit, residing now in Maui, HI.

www.ingramcontent.com/pod-product-compliance
Lightning Source LLC
Chambersburg PA
CBHW011747220426
43667CB00020B/2923